Running Against the Wind

Running Against the Wind

A Handbook for Presidents and Chancellors

Michael Wartell

ROWMAN & LITTLEFIELD
Lanham • Boulder • New York • London

Published by Rowman & Littlefield
A wholly owned subsidiary of The Rowman & Littlefield Publishing Group, Inc.
4501 Forbes Boulevard, Suite 200, Lanham, Maryland 20706
www.rowman.com

Unit A, Whitacre Mews, 26-34 Stannary Street, London SE11 4AB

Copyright © 2016 by Michael Wartell

All rights reserved. No part of this book may be reproduced in any form or by any electronic or mechanical means, including information storage and retrieval systems, without written permission from the publisher, except by a reviewer who may quote passages in a review.

British Library Cataloguing in Publication Information Available

Library of Congress Cataloging-in-Publication Data

Names: Wartell, Michael.
Title: Running against the wind: a handbook for presidents and chancellors.
Description: Lanham, Maryland : Rowman & Littlefield, 2016. | Includes bibliographical references and index.
Identifiers: LCCN 2016010397 (print) | LCCN 2016013796 (ebook) | ISBN 9781475828276 (cloth : alk. paper) | ISBN 9781475828283 (pbk. : alk. paper) | ISBN 9781475828290 (Electronic)
Subjects: LCSH: College presidents--United States--Handbooks, manuals, etc. | Universities and colleges--United States--Administration--Handbooks, manuals, etc.
Classification: LCC LB2341 .W37 2016 (print) | LCC LB2341 (ebook) | DDC 378.1/11--dc23
LC record available at http://lccn.loc.gov/2016010397

Printed in the United States of America

Contents

Foreword		vii
Preface		ix
1	What Is a University President/Chancellor and What Does He or She Do?	1
2	Getting the Job: What's the Process?	7
3	You've Got the Job: What Do You Do Now?	17
4	The Structure of Institutions: Who's in Charge?	23
5	Dealing with Internal Constituencies	29
6	The Board: Trustees, Visitors, and Otherwise	43
7	Dealing with External Constituencies	47
8	Institutional Structures, Organizations, and Responsibilities	61
9	In General	81
10	Case Studies	99
Conclusion		105

Foreword

It would be hard to find a book to be a more compelling read for a prospective college or university president/chancellor than Michael Wartell's *Running Against the Wind: A Handbook for Presidents and Chancellors*. What is in this book is not only knowledge but also wisdom, and the latter is almost always bought dearly and in short supply. Furthermore, it only comes from deep personal experience and penetrating self-reflection over an extended time period. In graceful directness and expansive but succinct breadth, this volume rivals John Gardner's (1990) classic *On Leadership*.

I was also struck by a phenomenon outlined by famed British physical chemist Michael Polyani, who did research in thermodynamics, X-ray analysis, and reaction kinetics. Polyani spoke about how scientists developed a kind of sixth sense about their work and about which "the grounds of both science and art were neither objective nor subjective, but personal" (Prosch, 1986, p. 262). Such meanings were beyond quantification and measurement and based on "tacit coefficients" (Prosch, 1986). Polyani called these meanings *tacit knowledge*, where we know more than we can tell. What is amazing about this book is that Michael Wartell has been able to plumb from his own reservoir of experience the nuggets of his own tacit knowledge and share them with his readers.

Finally, as someone who spent a brief time with Dr. Wartell in his administration at Indiana University–Purdue University Fort Wayne as his vice-chancellor of academic affairs (1996–1998) and witnessed his leadership on a daily basis, I can say his vision, courage, creativity, and ability to sense the major issues quickly and act decisively comprised the essence of superb leadership in action. As someone who now teaches educational leadership I'm not sure those attributes can be taught, but they can be learned. This book is a wonderful opportunity to acquire that learning. I think that Michael Wartell's advice on leading is the embodiment of what Paul Keating (2004), the twenty-fourth prime minister of Australia, defined as leadership when he said:

> Leadership is about interpreting the future to the present; having the ability to see over the horizon; letting those wider coordinates inform one's thinking. Giving one the ability to move forward more profoundly, and by moving forward I mean not having one foot in the safe house of incrementalism. (p. 1)

I commend this volume on leadership regarding the pivotal position of chancellor/president of a college or university with the greatest confidence that the reader will not only find it an invaluable and inspiring resource, but will come back to the advice and insights on these pages again and again.

Fenwick W. English:
R. Wendell Eaves Senior Distinguished Professor of Educational Leadership, School of Education, The University of North Carolina at Chapel Hill

REFERENCES

Gardner, J. (1990). *On leadership.* New York: Harper & Row.

Keating, P. (2004). Human resource management: The role of leadership. Address given to the Australian Human Resources Institute. Melbourne, May 11, 2004. Retrieved from http://www.keating.org.au/shop/item/human-resource-management-the-role-fleadership-11-May-2004.

Polanyi, M. (1967). *The tacit dimension.* New York: Doubleday.

Prosch, H. (1986). *Michael Polyani: A critical exposition.* Albany: State University of New York Press.

Preface

In track and field competition, when a race competitor sets a record and the breeze is at his or her back, the feat is recorded with the caveat that it was wind assisted, an admission that the accomplishment was not quite as heroic as it might have been. In similar competition, when a record is set while running against the wind, no mention is made in the annals of the race of what may have been a truly heroic feat, requiring much more energy and effort than is immediately obvious.

Presidents/chancellors of universities are treated similarly. They work in a diverse environment of constituent groups, each of which has its own purposes and goals. In rare cases, a president/chancellor leads an institutional change or improvement that is supported by all constituencies. And the accomplishment is treated like setting a wind-assisted record.

However, in most cases, changes or improvements are accomplished in an environment where some constituent groups support the change and others oppose it. In a few cases, needed improvements are managed while most constituent groups oppose them. And the leader is credited with little more than doing his or her job, while the energy, effort, and capability required to run against the constituent wind is largely ignored.

Presidents/chancellors function and work in a swirl of constituencies, each one working toward its own ends. Leading and managing in this environment requires energy, effort, capability, and patience coupled with an awareness of and sensitivity to the needs of the constituent groups.

When first appointed, many presidents/chancellors are blissfully unaware of the complexity of their environment. In previous positions as deans or vice presidents, their purview was limited, and in many cases, they focused on one or two constituencies. A vice president for academic affairs may have focused on faculty and students, having little interaction with donors, the community, or even students. A student affairs VP might have focused on students, professional staff, and the community, having little interaction with faculty and elected officials.

Many newly appointed presidents/chancellors also suffer from being poorly acquainted with the complex responsibilities of the position because the president/chancellor with whom they worked in their previous job paid little attention to their professional development and shared little information with them. The learning curve in these situations is steep and dangerous and may account for the short tenure of many campus leaders.

Of course some new presidents/chancellors come to the job from another presidency/chancellorship. The danger for them is that the environment in the new position is so different that they are unprepared for it. They may also be moving from a smaller to a larger institution and are surprised by the scale of the operation. Imagine the culture shock resulting from moving from a university having fewer students than the new institution has employees.

Whatever the situation and environment, a useful approach to succeeding is to clearly define the job and its expectations, understand the environment and constituencies and their relationships, and imagine your reaction to the situations that may confront you. And realize that, for most of your tenure, you will be running against the wind.

ONE

What Is a University President/Chancellor and What Does He or She Do?

No matter how small or large a college or university is, the responsibilities of its president/chancellor are broad and complex but can be distilled to comprise two fundamental issues: garnering the resources necessary for the institution to accomplish its mission and managing their use in the most efficient and effective manner.

It sounds simple, doesn't it? However, to succeed, any president or chancellor must account for an increasing spectrum of variables and be accountable to a broadening collection of constituencies. Most people knowledgeable about higher education will assign the above responsibilities to "management" and point out that collecting and expending resources is simply mechanical and will not guarantee the growth or success of an institution. But to collect resources and manage their deployment a president/chancellor must engender the support of both internal and external constituencies. Such action requires leadership, so a president/chancellor must lead as well as manage. However, often there is uncertainty in defining leadership and its qualities.

What must a university leader do? First, a leader must develop a shared vision within and without the organization. Vision for an institution is your view of what the institution could be. It might include more campus land, more buildings, residential facilities where there are now few or none, better interaction with the community, more externally funded research, a more welcoming campus environment, a larger endowment, a more successful athletic program, national prominence, or any of a number of other issues. It could also include increased graduation rates, enhanced student retention, and better employer and employee relations. It could be all of the above, but it might be even more grandiose.

Imagine a junior college becoming a four-year institution, a master's comprehensive institution becoming a research-intensive campus offering PhDs, or Haverford College aspiring to join the Big Ten athletic conference. All of these improvements constitute visions for an institution, but they don't happen just because the president/chancellor promulgates an idea. They can't happen without the support of a significant part of the institutional community. That's what shared vision is about.

Organizations are more likely to grow and thrive when those in the organization and the constituencies of that organization understand, accept, and can move in a common direction. But universities and colleges are uniquely full of bright, articulate people who, by and large, believe that they can run the organization better than its current president/chancellor and who might agree on broad goals but agree on few specific ones and fewer means of reaching them. So creating a shared vision is especially important and difficult in this environment.

Shared vision results from your convincing constituents that the end state you imagine is good for the institution and for them. Improvements can also occur in the opposite way whereby you agree with the vision a group of constituencies has for the institution. But no matter how it happens, the parties involved must agree and support the vision and direction.

Within and supporting that shared vision must be a set of shared values. Organizations do not function well if values such as quality, competence, integrity, effectiveness, efficiency, diversity, respect, transparency, commitment, and excellence are not a part of the fabric of the organizational belief system. And they function especially poorly if parts of the organization act within the value system and others do not.

Further, the president/chancellor must be a role model, visible in a commitment to the vision and values of the institution and consistent in behavior surrounding that set of beliefs. If the institution's leader is not viewed as committed to the vision and values, why should anyone else in the organization embrace them?

But what are the components of successful leadership? Articles about leading organizations and characteristics and behaviors of leaders have been prominent in the media and academic literature for many years. In those venues, pundits, authors, and motivational speakers who have led organizations no larger than a two-person office are fully capable of articulating broad-ranging and authoritative opinions detailing the how-tos of leadership. And most come to similar conclusions about leaders embodying integrity, good communication, charisma, vision, intelligence, energy, and several other descriptors.

But it is not at all clear to me whether, together or separately, those traits are what leadership is about or that exhibiting them necessarily results in successful leadership.

Unquestionably, effective, successful leaders must possess some combination of the traits listed, and we could argue about which ones are more important. But there is an overarching attitude, approach, or belief system that determines whether a leader is effective. And it's not a concept that easily succumbs to a single-word description. However, it's possible to describe the approach by describing its parts and then attempting to find a simple description to be used in that context.

So what characterizes successful leadership? A successful leader must believe that the growth and well-being of the organization or institution is primary and far more important than the leader's personal needs. The leader must accept responsibility for the lives and livelihoods of the organization's employees. The leader must understand that realization of students' and staff's goals and satisfaction is central to the organization's success.

But that's not enough. Successfully leading also includes modeling behavior that convinces those within the organization and whom the organization serves that the belief is authentic. Stated even more directly, good leadership is authentically assuming personal responsibility for all aspects of the organization's responsibilities and truly owning your decisions. In this way, individuals at every level within the institution can better accept their own responsibilities in support of the campus.

And this is what leadership is about. So although developing shared vision and values and modeling behavior consistent with the vision and values is difficult, the most daunting aspect of leadership is communicating the ideas, beliefs, and directions to constituencies whose own goals, values, needs, and beliefs may be both different and uncertain. And that communication must be consistent, constant, and clear. Because in institutions of higher education the most damning and damaging labels affixed to a president/chancellor are "dishonest," "disingenuous," and "opaque" in his or her dealings.

But in a college or university setting, modeling the behavior and communicating are still insufficient, because developing "shared" vision and values requires not only constant, consistent, clear communication but also a reputation for listening, considering multiple inputs and ideas in solving problems, and respecting those who are proffering those ideas. So where the "shared" aspect of shared vision is concerned, the most damning and damaging labels are "overbearing," "autocratic," and "insensitive."

Thus, a president has a multifaceted responsibility, having to manage resources productively and simultaneously leading, herding the "cats and dogs" that comprise the employees and constituencies of the university toward a vision and goals that may or may not, initially, be fully embraced.

WHAT IS THE MOTIVATION FOR BECOMING AND REMAINING A PRESIDENT/CHANCELLOR?

It is sometimes difficult to understand why academics aspire to lead universities, because, once in the position, so many complain about the responsibilities, the politics, the constituencies, and the primary actors in the college or university—the faculty and students. The problems facing universities are complex and well publicized, so anyone aspiring to a leadership position ought to understand clearly exactly what they are getting into. However, several internal motivators come into play.

Some are attracted to the power, which is illusory at best. Some enjoy the adulation that comes with lofty positions, but adulation can turn to denigration in the blink of an eye. Some simply want a higher salary and perquisites, but except for a few prominent universities, salaries are not commensurate with responsibilities. Some love the satisfaction of continually improving an institution, but find that it's very hard work. And some just believe that they can do the job better than anyone else, an attitude that your faculty will attempt to strip from you almost immediately.

For most, the motivations are a combination of these and others. It is important that you examine your own motivations, because your personal measures of success will result from a mapping of accomplishments against motivations. And whether you wish to continue in a position often depends on the attitudes of constituents as well as your own feelings. Remember that the average tenure of a university CEO is approximately five years, hardly enough time to really change an institution or even complete the most rudimentary of plans.

As the result of the realization that tenures are relatively short, many presidents/chancellors simply aspire to survive after two or three years. Like turtles, they seldom stick their necks out, retreating into their shells at the first sign of trouble. Such behavior includes not being seen on campus to avoid questioning, sending surrogates to institutional events where the CEO should have appeared, and avoiding public places where constituents might gather. As constituents recognize the behavior, they become less and less supportive and can exert significant influence in shortening the CEO's tenure.

While some CEOs operate for years in survival mode, they are seldom respected and their institutions are more likely barely surviving rather than thriving. No matter what the situation, it is better to confront the issues directly rather than to retreat and avoid. You may not survive the encounter, but at least you will retain your integrity. And you are more likely to be able to leave on your own terms.

TWO

Getting the Job

What's the Process?

The most common professional road to a presidency or chancellorship is relatively well defined and follows along an academic career. One earns a terminal degree, serves time as a faculty member, becomes a department chair, obtains a deanship, snags a provostship or vice presidency, and then applies for presidencies/chancellorships as they become available. In rare cases, one or another of the steps is skipped, or a staff position (assistant this or associate that) is held along the way. And in even rarer cases, a president has had a career in development, student affairs, industry, or even, heaven forbid, politics.

However, the academic path seems to be the preferred approach. It also seems to be the most successful approach. The success rate (tenures lasting more than five years) of individuals who are elevated to the position of chancellor or president from deanships or below seems lower than those who follow the more traditional path. Scott Cowen at Tulane, having been a business school dean, is the counterexample since he has had a lengthy and successful tenure. Politicians (governors, senators, and the like) have enjoyed either wildly successful or wildly unsuccessful experiences.

But from whatever stone (position) one might step into a presidency, it is necessary to identify openings. Such openings are commonly advertised in media outlets such as the *Chronicle of Higher Education* or the *Hispanic Outlook* higher education publication, or any of a number of others. Perusal of these outlets should lead one to a group of positions for which requirements meet the applicant's qualifications.

Ordinarily, it is futile (though not impossible) to aspire to positions outside the applicant's experiences. For example, applicants from community colleges will seldom be considered for leadership in baccalaureate institutions. And careers in baccalaureate and master's institutions will seldom lead to leadership in doctoral granting institutions. Similarly, it is uncommon for those having careers in private institutions to move to public institutions and vice versa. Thus, in spite of academia's celebration of diversity, knowing your place in the higher education hierarchy can save you frustration and disappointment.

When searching for a president/chancellor, those responsible, whether board, search committee, or search firm, will imagine the characteristics of their next leader. If asked, they will often respond that a new leader should come from an institution of similar size, mission, and characteristics in general.

If the searching institution emphasizes research, many believe that coming from an institution that emphasizes teaching will immediately disqualify a candidate. If the searching institution emphasizes teaching, the prevailing mantra will be that coming from a research institution causes candidates to be insensitive to the rigor and value of teaching. This attitude is especially obvious in church-affiliated schools, where a belief prevails that the leader must be a practicing member of whatever sect is in charge.

Almost as rigid, but not quite so, is the belief that having a career in a public institution automatically disqualifies one for service at a private one. It is felt that especially where donor relations, board interaction, and budget development are concerned, any applicant from a public institution is unqualified. Similar beliefs surround athletics. Applicants from institutions having "small-time" athletics are viewed as incapable of dealing with one supporting "big-time" athletics. The converse also occurs. An applicant having experience with large athletic programs can be seen as overqualified for institutions having lower-level programs.

Once a position or cache of appropriate positions is identified, then the application or nomination process begins. These days, the initial application and interview processes require submission of a letter of interest and résumé and are often managed by executive search firms hired by the institution. Fewer are managed by the institution itself. So applications and nominations are sent to the search firms where candidates' files are initially winnowed.

Credentials are often rejected for the most arcane reasons. Misspellings, poor grammar, and inserting the wrong institution into the application letter will not be helpful to a candidacy. There have been so many instances of search committees rejecting candidates for these reasons that it is easy to overlook them. So, misspellings on résumés and curricula vitae of journal names and common words occur often. You'd think the spell-checker was written in another language. Verb and subject agreement, "there/their," "bear/bare," "fair/fare," "then" as "than," and other misuses are also common and not covered by the spell-checker.

And finally, using an already written letter of interest while forgetting to change the institutional name is an understandable but also unforgivable sin. Padded, vague, or incomplete résumés are also game changers.

Little irritates a search committee or firm more than discovering a major negative aspect of the candidate's past that was omitted or glossed over in a résumé. The basic advice in this case is be honest. It's much better to be imperfect than to be a liar. Do not leave gaps in your employment history. Don't fill your résumé with university committees on which you've served. Leave Rotary and other service club speeches out. In short, your résumé should comprise significant professional accomplishments and little else. Rejection at this point may have less to do with an applicant's qualifications and more to do with résumé quality, uncertainty about the candidate's experience, discovery of misleading aspects of a résumé, and misreading of the résumé.

In most searches, the winnowing process is handled by the campus search committee or a search firm. So it pays to call the representative of the search firm or the search committee chair to ensure that your candidacy is "top of mind" and that your existence is "top of memory." In many instances, the representative or search chair will share valuable information about the situation at the institution, your competitiveness for the position, and a description of the type of person sought for the position.

It is important to keep in mind that the search firm's goal is to swell the candidate pool and more encouragement than is warranted might be provided. So don't be fooled by the affability or the enthusiasm of the representative. He or she is just doing a job.

The search committee chair will be more genuine. Among the information that search firms or search committee chairs might share is an assessment of the campus climate (open, repressive, depressed, etc.), whether the new CEO is expected to be a change agent or to pour oil on the water, if there are internal candidates, and even whether you are competitive in the candidate pool. (However, don't expect a search firm representative to be entirely truthful about the last issue.) This information can help you assess whether you should apply at all or take the entire process seriously. The information can also be helpful in ensuring success in future interviews.

Further, unbeknownst to you or the rest of the world, the institution may already have a favored candidate. Often the search firm will know but will never share the information with you. Sometimes the firm will discover later that a candidate is favored and will be embarrassed by the discovery, but don't expect an apology or that the firm will return the institution's fee. Internal candidates (although this could be positive or negative), friends of board members, or applicants from sister campuses all may have an advantage in the search process. Once again, the sum of the fingers on both hands is inadequate to count the number of times there has been a "most favored candidate" throughout the search.

To the extent possible, it is important to enter into searches fully aware that such candidates might exist. Finding out as much as possible about the search process and campus environment can save undue disappointment in the final outcome.

As described previously, once the applicant pool is identified, winnowing of files is undertaken solely by the search firm, solely by the search committee, by some combination of the two, or rarely by some other arcane method or individual. However this is done, the result is usually a short list of eight to ten candidates who best fit the position description. Ordinarily, these five to ten are then invited to a Draconian exercise known as "airport" interviews. These are one- to two-hour encounters that include the candidate, the search committee, and/or a representative of the search firm. The goal of such interviews is to reduce the candidate pool to a small group of finalists.

The format of these interviews varies only slightly from one institution to another and usually consists of the candidates being asked a scripted list of questions always asked in the same order by the same member of the search committee. The questions are almost always the same:

- Describe your administrative style.
- Define shared governance.
- How can administrative teams best be built?
- Describe your experience in private fund-raising.
- Describe the process that led to your largest gift.
- Take us through a typical day in your life.
- What are your beliefs about diversity and how have you acted on them?
- Do you have experience with collective bargaining?
- How do you make decisions and with whom do you consult?
- Is athletics important to a university?
- How can you build community support?
- Do you believe in sustainability?
- Describe your successes and failures and what you've learned from them.
- What in your past experience uniquely qualifies you for this job?
- Tell us what you do for fun.
- Explain your definition of an "engaged university."
- Have you dealt with collective bargaining during your career?
- What experience have you had with strategic planning?
- Describe the role of research in a teaching institution.

However, no matter what questions are asked, who's doing the asking, or what the mood of the interview is, these encounters are beauty contests.

After all, how much can be learned from an hour's discussion among fifteen people using only the candidate's résumé as a guide? Up to this point, no referencing has been done, and the only information beyond the résumé comes from Google, search committee colleagues' contacts, and personal knowledge. So the search committee bases its judgment on what is little more than a first impression.

While many of a search committee's questions may be scripted and much can be learned from those scripted questions, the unscripted ones are especially enlightening. Sometimes the questions asked indicate that the candidate's résumé was never read. Sometimes they indicate that the questioner has overlooked obvious characteristics of the candidate. Sometimes they are embarrassingly inappropriate.

The structure of the committee can also be instructive. If the committee is rigidly structured with little representation from faculty and staff, but all unions are carefully represented, that is a good indication of what can and cannot be accomplished during a CEO's tenure. If the committee comprises a significant number of board members, it's an indication of the level of trust existing on the campus. If there are few women or minorities on the committee, there is insensitivity to diversity. If there is sparse faculty representation, shared governance should be questioned. The structure and behavior of the search committee can be an accurate indicator of who's in control and the mood of the campus.

It is also interesting that these airport interviews are usually scheduled for five to ten candidates and spread over two days. As a result, if a candidate is scheduled at the beginning, the committee is often disorganized, attempting to find a rhythm, and suffers memory fade by the end of the series of interviews. If the candidate is scheduled at the end, the committee is often tired, has become bored with the process, and can appear to be just going through the motions.

Encountering a committee at the beginning of the process, a candidate often finds members confused about who is to ask which question. Then when mistakes in questioning are made, the embarrassment often results in a recovery period during which committee members stop listening to answers. In this situation, it is best to speak especially simply and clearly, repeating an answer if committee members' attention seems to have wandered. Observe them carefully to understand your environment.

It is important not to tailor answers to fit what a committee might want to hear, but to remain sensitive to the committee's mood. Being among the last candidates to interview, an applicant may encounter committee members who are "heavy lidded" during the interview. While one could assume that my answers bored them, it is more probable that they were simply exhausted at the end of the interview process. No matter what the condition of the committee, the best advice is to be energetic, even passionate about your beliefs, straightforward, and honest, and don't give answers that are too lengthy, but fully answer the question. Otherwise, someone might think you are all talk and no action.

At the end of the interview, time is usually allotted for the candidate to ask questions. It is impossible to guess what sort of questions are expected, but steering clear of the following questions is probably good advice:

- How do you expect to attract anyone to an institution this far in the boonies?
- The unrest on your campus seems toxic. How do you expect anyone to deal with it?
- Your academic reputation is abysmal. How do you plan to improve?
- How could you have allowed your physical facilities to deteriorate so much?
- Your financial situation is depressing. Do you see any way of improving it?
- The search committee seems depressed. Is the situation that bad at the institution?

Rather, questions that might be productive are:

- What are the major challenges facing the institution and how do you rank them?
- Does the institution welcome change or is change viewed negatively?
- How is the institution reacting to national trends such as globalization, use of technology, and output metrics?
- Has the institution embraced assessment and/or strategic planning?
- How has the institution fared in these challenging financial times?
- What are the institution's aspirations or "stretch" goals?

While it can be argued that searching through résumés to find the best five to ten candidates from a large candidate pool may not yield the most qualified semifinalists or those who fit best, a similar argument can be made concerning the method for gleaning the best three to five finalists from the five to ten.

Once the finalists are chosen, unless the institution considers itself above the common practice, the candidates are ordinarily invited to a campus interview wherein the many constituencies of the institution participate in serial questioning of the candidate. These are often marathon affairs designed more to test the candidates' stamina rather than their experience, intelligence, flexibility, leadership skills, or innovativeness.

The only advice appropriate to this part of the interview is to be open, transparent, and honest. In these interviews, you should expose exactly what you are, because if you are chosen, any dishonesty will be immediately obvious and you will be on the road to failure. Also, it is important to look presidential/chancellorial. Often interview committees both in public and private sectors, discount candidates because they didn't look presidential.

Describe big-picture concepts and use previous experiences only as examples. Further, make clear exactly what you have accomplished. Try not to take credit for what others have done. The pronoun "I" should seldom appear in discussion. "We," meaning "the team," should get the credit.

It is important to separate appearances over which you have control and those over which you do not. Dressing appropriately, being aware of your own distracting mannerisms, and ensuring that you make eye contact are among controllable behaviors. And you will be judged on them appropriately. Whether you are tall or short, slender or heavy, blonde or brunette are uncontrollable factors on which committee members may judge you. They are obviously inappropriate, and if used, make employment at the institution unattractive.

Similarly, sounding presidential is important. If asked about your commitment to diversity, don't simply give examples of policies and programs in which you have participated. Explain that diversity is a core value for you and your belief in the power of diversity is unswerving; then give examples. In this way, you can demonstrate a deeper belief in and a more global understanding of the subject. Similar responses are appropriate when asked about liberal arts education, integrity, flexibility, shared governance, academic freedom, and a broad range of other subjects.

Also, realize that your spouse or partner will be a part of the interview too. In some cases, the spouse or partner will be expected to accompany you at every step of the process. In others, their presence will be expected only at on-campus interviews. It is important to understand that the institution is hiring not only a president/chancellor but also a team. Your spouse or partner and even your entire immediate family may be expected to be a presence on campus.

Finally, once chosen, cut the best deal you can because it is only in rare instances that boards or bosses see your obvious value once you're on board. And unless you are able to make yourself irreplaceable (and few of us can), you are not going to get another chance.

APPLICATION VERSUS NOMINATION VERSUS REFERRAL

When determining how to apply for a position, several options are possible. Since president/chancellor position openings are published in the *Chronicle of Higher Education*, the *New York Times*, and many other media outlets, one could simply apply to the appropriate official or ask a colleague for a nomination. In some cases, search firms will consult their list of potential candidates and call to request an application. In still other cases a board member, elected official, or other institutional official might solicit interest.

Consider the effectiveness of each of these paths. Unsolicited applications are about as effective as cold sales calls. Unless the applicant's reputation precedes him or her (Nobel Prize, Pulitzer Prize, definitive body of work in an important discipline), the application has little chance of being noticed unless the search committee or firm is especially diligent. Nominations invite greater visibility depending on the reputation of the writer and the compelling nature of the letter. In most cases, a nomination is best coming from a colleague, at least at the vice president/vice-chancellor level.

In either case, a call to the chair of the search committee and/or the designated search firm official can better introduce the applicant, determine whether the institutional parameters indicate a fit, and raise recognition to top of mind. This approach can backfire if the officials involved are too busy or arrogant, or just plain unwilling to deal with the situation. However, in most cases, it will have a positive effect.

If invited to apply by a search firm, at least two scenarios are possible. Either the search firm believes that there is a genuine confluence of applicant credentials and institutional needs or the firm has promised the institution a specific applicant pool size and many applications are just fodder for the search's cannon. The latter situation is easy to avoid if one engages in an honest evaluation of institutional fit and comparison to other applicants' credentials. But it's difficult to recognize if the search firm is complicit in advancing a preferred candidate.

If a board member, elected official, or university administrator requests an application, unless you are genuinely uninterested, update your résumé. You have a leg up.

THE RISK OF CANDIDACY

Being a candidate in a search for a president/chancellor carries with it multiple risks.

1. The chances of confidentiality being maintained are slim to none. Whether a search committee member, a board member, or anyone else slips and divulges sensitive information or the search is totally open, the candidacy will become public.
2. In the short term, direct reports and others in the university will question your loyalty, commitment, and ability to do your job. Community members and media will simply ask questions. Donors will wonder whether they should contribute further to the projects you are championing.

3. In the short and long term, the board will question your commitment and may, in the end, discontinue your service. On the other hand, they may also make an offer that includes increased salary, extended tenure, and expanded perquisites. Risks sometimes reap rewards.

Sometimes public knowledge of a search can turn sour for candidates.

1. Imagine a president who allows a vice president to participate in only one job search, after which, if the VP is unsuccessful, he or she returns to the faculty.
2. Imagine a president/chancellor in the same pool of candidates for a position where his or her vice president/vice-chancellor is also a candidate. If discovery of the situation is a surprise, trust can almost never be rebuilt, especially if one or the other is insecure.
3. Imagine a donor discovering a president/chancellor is involved in a search, losing confidence in the commitment of the president/chancellor, and canceling a seven-figure gift.

Each of these situations is possible. The best approach to minimizing risk is to carefully assess the personalities and attitudes involved, explore hypotheticals with those who might cause the greatest negative consequences, be open about your intentions, and decide on the most appropriate path.

THE SEARCH PROCESS AND COMMITTEE BEHAVIOR

Presidential searches and search committees can be nightmarish. Consider several examples of situations that can and do occur and should warn candidates away from an institution.

1. Imagine a presidential search where two finalists are identified after an extended process. The final hurdle is a televised board interview where each candidate is interviewed separately, after which a decision would be reached. During the televised final board interview, board members and one candidate are on a first-name basis. The other candidate is treated formally. When the final decision is announced the board chair proudly states that he has known the preferred candidate ever since the board chair had met his current wife, and as a result, he believes him to be the superior candidate.
2. Imagine a search process whereby the acting president (a candidate for the position) is responsible for search logistics and ensures that other candidates for on-campus visits are housed in hotels that are far below decent standards to increase their discomfort in the interview.

3. Imagine a large search committee comprising seven union members (one from each of the collective bargaining units), two trustees, a student, two community representatives, an executive-level administrator, a mid-level administrator, the university legal counsel, and almost as an afterthought, two faculty members.
4. Imagine an interview with a diverse search committee where only board members ask questions.
5. Imagine a search for the president of an institution within a system where the search committee chair is the president of a sister (and possibly rival) institution in the system. What a potential conflict of interest.
6. Imagine a search process whereby all of the presidential candidates visit the campus simultaneously and meet one another randomly throughout the visit.
7. Imagine an airport interview during which the faculty representatives and administrators argue with one another about the goals and mission of the institution.
8. Imagine an interview dinner with board members where several drink to the point of incoherence.
9. Imagine an interview during which members of the search committee ask about age, family ethnicity, and opinion on right to life. Further, on the question of religion, when a committee member asks about church attendance and it is suggested that the question is inappropriate, he responds, "It's alright. I'm a minister!"

THREE
You've Got the Job
What Do You Do Now?

Once an institution chooses a campus CEO, its normal first actions include hosting a press conference to announce the choice. At that event, the new president/chancellor speaks. That first opportunity is crucial. An often quoted bit of wisdom is that you have only one chance to make a first impression. Internalize this bit of advice, because at this event (and at many subsequent events), you can either damage yourself massively or set the stage for a successful tenure at the institution. So don't blow it! Here are several suggestions:

1. Don't make factual errors. Doing so makes you appear not to have cared enough to get your facts straight, and fact checking takes little time and effort. Typical errors include misstating enrollments, mentioning programs that are not offered at the institution, under- or overstating the budget, and making nonfactual statements about athletic accomplishments.
2. Ensure that you don't mispronounce any names or words in your presentation. Making such errors indicates a lack of simple preparatory work. Few things irritate individuals more than mispronouncing their names. Well-known individuals such as elected officials and system chancellors are especially sensitive. And nothing makes you appear more ignorant than mispronouncing common words such as "façade."
3. Be culturally aware. Either learn about on-campus and off-campus relationships and be sure that the information is accurate or don't bring up any of them. Attempts to look knowledgeable, if data are inaccurate, cement the opposite impression or result in making

unnecessary enemies. For example, in systems, fully understand the relationship between the system office and the campus before commenting or acting on it. If the system and campus have an arm's-length relationship, don't emphasize the importance of system interactions. Never suggest severing the tie to the system under any circumstance. And with respect to the athletic program, learn the campus and community attitudes before making any statement or describing policy intentions.

4. Thank people accurately and appropriately. This is good advice for any presentation. Thanking people who obviously don't deserve it or not thanking those who do can damage your reputation. By the way, the greater sin is thanking those who are undeserving because those who deserve the credit will inevitably have long memories and remaining unrecognized for hard work or good ideas will be especially galling to them.

5. Be short and to the point. No one wants to hear a long soliloquy at a news conference. Be especially careful about long descriptions of your family. It may be that close professional colleagues will care and the campus gossips will file the information away, but most listeners will not care and will be intolerant of the indulgence. It is important to remember that while this news conference is about your appointment, in the end it is about the institution. Emphasizing that can only enhance others' opinions of you. Also, appear confident and articulate in your delivery. You will be criticized if you appear unsure of yourself and your message. A halting presentation punctuated by "uhs" and "ums" will do you no good.

6. Set out a vision if you have one. It can be incredibly general, but it helps people to know that you've thought about direction for the organization and that you can communicate it simply. You're in charge! You're leading! Setting a general vision gives the impression that you know where you're going. And if you feel you're not informed enough to express a vision, share your values and the tenets on which your administration will be based. Your constituencies will expect at least that of you.

So much for the first news conference speech. Immediately after that, get involved with your new campus. Don't worry about when you start officially. For most constituencies, you start when you are announced. So nothing bespeaks a lack of commitment or caring more than indicating that, up until the moment you actually take over, you are uninterested in past, current, or future campus issues.

Ask for data in regard to the campus and study them. Meet with campus and community individuals and organizations to assess the culture and environment. In those meetings remember that your campus community comes first. Without their support, you have no platform from which to address the external community. Interact with students if they're around.

Make a special effort to meet with your direct reports both to acquaint them with you and to acquaint you with them. And be sure to communicate work-habit expectations (including your own) and protocol issues. If you have strong beliefs about work habits, interpersonal interactions, and office policies, protocols, and organization, communicate them! Others may not agree, but they will adapt to those aspects of your management style. However, be careful where you impose your personality quirks. Imagine a president who insists on having fruit available at every on-campus meeting. Subordinates will tolerate such "slightly off" behavior, but that president invited trouble by insisting that fruit be available at off-campus meetings hosted and paid for by others.

In these meetings, spend time listening to your new constituencies. It will be much easier for you to adapt to the culture, attitudes, and conditions of the institution and its constituencies than it is for them to adapt to you. You may have many good ideas for change, but they need to be introduced patiently or else you risk lethal backlash. And you can change institutional culture, but the institution needs to be led toward that change.

As you begin your new job, consider this. Unless you're working at a brand new university, someone else occupied the post before you. Loved or hated, revered or reviled, canonized or defamed, that person supported certain programs or projects, participated in events, and had characteristics that are well worth your notice. And no matter what opinion the constituencies had of your predecessor, there are bound to have been certain behaviors, events, and programs they too supported as well as certain ones they didn't.

It's in your best interest to figure out which are which, because in higher education institutions, change is the most difficult constant. If you can continue the positive and avoid falling victim to the negative, you can considerably ease your transition into the job and allow you, with appropriate speed, to place your own work on the institution.

During this introductory period, there is no such thing as overexposure. You need to be everywhere, convincing constituencies that you are open, accessible, and in the end, trustworthy. And always keep in mind that it's about the institution, not about you!

NEGOTIATING A DEAL

You're offered the job. Now consideration of salary, perquisites, retention bonuses, retirement plans, and anything else that might be part of a compensation package is appropriate. A few suggestions might help.

1. If the stakes are high enough and a formal, multidimensional contract is involved, hire a lawyer. The board that is hiring you is not working in your best interest. It is working for the institution. Remember that at public institutions, the parameters of an agreement must conform with law and policy, whereas at private institutions, the guidelines are much less rigid.
2. At many institutions, the salary is negotiable only within narrow limits. At others, there may be more flexibility, but keep in mind that other institutional employees are judging your character and greed will not become you.
3. Do not skimp on the contractual arrangements that allow you to be successful. Club memberships, entertainment budgets, travel arrangements, automobile and driver access, and professional assistance, among other things, will be invaluable in your interactions with donors and other supporters.
4. Exit arrangements are critical. Negotiate a clear arrangement.
5. Attempt to negotiate a clear separation of duties between you and the board.
6. If you have a "trailing spouse" and expect that person to be employed within the institution, ensure that the situation is covered in the initial agreement. Otherwise, if the person is hired later, you will be accused of nepotism.

THE FIRST IMPRESSION FAUX PAS SYNDROME

Imagine several first impressions with which you might not wish to be associated.

1. A president's first visit to campus includes a dinner with the board and search committee. The dinner is delayed more than an hour because the new appointee refuses to eat red meat even though plenty of vegetables are available in the original meal. The delay results from new ingredients being acquired and prepared.
2. During the first week of a new president's tenure, there is an opportunity to speak to a meeting of two hundred clerical and service staff. The president refuses, stating, "That's HR's job, not mine!"
3. A CEO is presented with a list of formal occasions where the institution is host. His or her first response is, "Clinton Kelly, Martha Stewart, and I have an agreement. They don't run universities and I don't entertain!"
4. The board presents its new executive with a personal gift consisting of an antique bit of memorabilia related to the college or university. The executive's response is, "I've got no use for junk like that!"

5. During an initial meeting with direct reports, the CEO states clearly that no personal or health problem will excuse failure to perform duties or missing meetings.
6. At university events, the new president/chancellor wears clothing bearing the colors of his or her previous institution.

These are just some examples, but they really happened. Common sense will help you avoid the most damaging ones, and many colleagues will attribute the minor gaffs to eccentricity. But eccentricities are cumulative and indulging in too many will label you as "kooky."

FOUR

The Structure of Institutions

Who's in Charge?

Determining where the power lies in any organization, whether academic or otherwise, is central to determining how to lead and/or manage the organization. In an academic institution, the most obvious power center is the board of trustees, visitors, supervisors, or whatever. How its power and authority are manifested is determined, in the main, by the structure of the institution and/or system of which it is a part.

Consider, first, private institutions. They are ultimately overseen by boards. How individuals are chosen to serve is an important test of their function, as is the size of the board. If the board membership is self-determining and perpetuating, electing its own members without input from the campus CEO, then it operates independently and is unlikely to be influenced by anything but the performance of the CEO and the personal biases of the members. If, on the other hand, the campus CEO influences the choice of individual board members, it is more likely that personal relationships among board members and the CEO can also be influential.

Some board members may be elected by alumni and must therefore answer to that constituency.

Whichever situation prevails, unless they break state or federal laws or incur the wrath of state or regional accrediting agencies (as was the case with the Adelphi University board), their authority is unchallenged within the college or university. And the president/chancellor retaining their support is central to retaining his or her position.

Size of board is important as well. If the board is large, it is less likely to be involved in day-to-day operations or to engage in concerted efforts except in extreme situations.

Public institution oversight is different. First, board members can be chosen in several ways. In some cases they are gubernatorial or other political appointments. In others, they are elected by alumni. In still others, they are chosen by general election. There are even some who serve ex officio. Many boards are composed of combinations of these types of members.

But however they are chosen, they answer to external authority in ways that board members of private institutions often do not. If chosen by the governor, they can be heavily influenced by his or her personal beliefs or political leanings. If chosen by general election, they must be constantly aware of the general political climate and public opinion of their actions. If elected by alumni, they must pay attention to satisfying alumni expectations.

But public boards are influenced by more than their immediate constituencies. Since legislatures are responsible for significant fractions of public institutions' budgets, board members must concern themselves with the opinions of state legislators and, further, with a host of opinions of other elected officials, local, state, and federal. In addition, since public opinion influences elected officials, board members are sensitive to the attitudes and beliefs of the general public.

Thus, to retain board support, the president/chancellor must maintain positive relationships not only with board members but also with his or her constituencies. Thus, in deciding how to develop relationships with those who are the overriding authorities in an institution, the president/chancellor of the private institution deals with less complexity than the CEO of a public institution.

A variation of the public model is the large public system. If individual institutions have their own boards, then the public model applies to each. If, however, there is only one board for the entire system, then all of the constituencies become influential and, in addition, the CEO must concern himself or herself with the status of his or her institution with the board. If there is one or more favored institutions within the system, then the relationship of the CEO with the board and with other system CEOs becomes even more complex.

Whatever structure exists, the campus CEO must view the relationship with the board as critical to his or her moving the institution forward. Then, with that realization, the CEO must develop strong relationships with all of the constituencies that might influence the board.

Internal centers of power are less obvious and their relationships are more complex. Whether public or private, most academic organizations share governance through a combination of academic senates and committees representing other staff types. CEOs disrespect these groups at their peril since they provide bully pulpits for those with strongly held opinions of all types. In some institutions, these organized groups work in concert toward advancing the institution. In others they work in concert against the CEO or governing board. In still others, they have difficulty working together at all. Determining their relationships is primary to a CEO's ability to lead.

Further, and obviously, it is important to develop relationships with individuals who are respected on campus or who are in a position to sway opinions. Few organizations thrive on rumors to the extent that academic organizations do, and using individuals with whom you can communicate and make widely known your point of view is important.

And finally, don't overlook the power of the clerical staff as opinion makers on a campus or in any organization. Their beliefs about your behavior, values, and honesty can be integral to your success or failure.

CULTIVATING POWER CENTERS

As campus CEO, you must decide how to allocate your time and attention to on-campus and off-campus groups to achieve your goals for the institution. You must also determine what approaches are most effective and to which groups to allocate your time.

The board will be both your most important support group and your most dangerous adversary. While they have an emotional investment in your success because they appointed you, they can shorten your tenure if relations with them, campus conditions, or any of a number of other situations begin to sour. While there are many circumstances that you cannot control, your contact and relationship with the board is manageable and can ease difficult situations.

Cultivation of the board requires that you know as much about their personal and business situations as you can, their intentions with respect to board service and the institution, and whether each individual supported your appointment. It is intelligence gathering at its purest. Invite them to campus events, play golf and cards with them, engage their families. Pay special attention to local board members because they will be most vulnerable to being influenced by rumors generated on the campus and in the community. Never show disrespect for any board member's person or ideas.

Similar statements can be made about legislators and other elected officials. Serve on their advisory boards, offer campus intellectual resources in their support, and spend time at their events, but be careful about offering financial or emotional support to their campaigns unless you are in a position to contribute equally to both sides. Proffering financial support will result in your being labeled as being on one side or another whereas remaining politically neutral is a more prudent path.

Working with faculty requires developing relationships with individual faculty, the faculty senate, standing faculty committees, and ad hoc task forces and committees (Women's Studies, Athletics, Gay and Lesbian Alliance, and others). Where the senate is concerned, try to attend every meeting. You are leading the campus and the faculty members believe they are the most important entities on campus. Treat them that way.

When invited to a committee or task force, attend. Do not delegate the responsibility since that demeans the members, and they will not forget the slight. When you have chartered and appointed a task force, attend the first meeting and make it obvious that you believe their work is important.

Where cultivation of individual faculty is concerned, at whatever event you encounter them, make sure they believe you are genuinely interested in their research, families, and general condition. Your caring must be genuine, and you show that by remembering their names and important issues surrounding them. Also, the larger the campus, the more important these interactions are.

Nonacademic staff members need to be continually reminded that their jobs are important and that, without them, the campus could not function. Often, both faculty and students will minimize their importance. It falls to the CEO to debunk that myth and to maximize recognition of the contribution of the nonacademic staff.

Student senates are often loathe to have university administrators attend, so ensure that you are invited at least once or twice during the academic year. Make sure that your respect for the student justice system is well known. And show genuine concern for the condition of nonacademic student facilities.

Community organizations will inundate you with requests to speak. Accept as many as you can and adhere to the belief that no audience is too small. And, to the extent possible, offer campus advice and intellectual resources to the campus. Your support of and presence in the community will be repaid with both financial and emotional support.

For all constituencies, your visibility is important. Attend as many athletic events, fine arts events, lectures, and campus and community gatherings as possible. In addition, walk on the campus often. Drop in on faculty and administrators in their offices. Talk with people. Be seen. Pay as much attention to individuals as you can and make it obvious that you respect them, no matter what their station or position.

Here are several do's and don'ts.

Do:

1. Host informal board gatherings to better acquaint yourself with members.
2. When asked to provide refreshments for campus events, do so as much as possible.
3. Unless enjoined by law, expect to pay for breakfast, lunch, or dinner with elected officials.

4. Participate to the extent possible in community charitable and other fund-raising events.
5. Host appreciation events for campus employees as needed. Don't make them pay to participate.
6. Either annually or semiannually, host an appreciation event for third-shift workers.
7. At any reception, work the crowd.

Don't:

1. Consult your e-mail or messages at board meetings or dinners.
2. Lean under a table to hide consulting your e-mail or messages at a dinner.
3. Take phone calls during meetings unless a close relative has died.
4. When talking to individuals at receptions, let your eyes wander as if looking for the next more important conversation.
5. Let individuals at receptions monopolize your time unless they are making a seven-figure donation.
6. Make obvious that you are doing other work and not paying attention at meetings.

The basic rule is to be courteous and use common sense at all times. But you already knew that.

WHAT DOES THE ORGANIZATION CHART LOOK LIKE?

Many new presidents/chancellors assume their positions, picturing an institutional structure with which they are comfortable, which they believe works, or is the only one in which they can work, and expect to change structure almost immediately. If you are one of these, disabuse yourself of that approach immediately. Academic institutions are among the most conservative organizations in society, and they will resist change to the best of their ability.

So whether you believe that disciplinary clusters will serve the institution better than departments, that CEOs should have only a limited number of direct reports, that the organization should be flat rather than hierarchical, that a provost system is better than a vice-whatever system, or that any organizational change is immediately necessary, calm down and be patient. Making immediate changes will be viewed as inappropriate by most constituencies and may imperil your tenure.

On the other hand, if the board insists on such change, find a subtle way to make that known or insist that the board take the credit and follow the board's mandate.

It is important to keep in mind that no organizational structure is inherently good or bad. It is the quality of the people occupying positions in the structure and their ability to work together that ultimately determine the success or failure of an organization. Making structural changes seldom results in a change in organizational performance. So wait until the organization develops trust in you and your behavior before suggesting structural changes.

A similar argument can be made about changing personnel immediately on assuming a position. Unless an employee is universally distrusted, is widely deemed incompetent, or has committed a crime, he or she will have developed supporters and detractors during his or her tenure. And such an employee's immediate removal will engender an atmosphere of fear and unfairness, which will not endear you to the campus. Most employees see their loyalty to the campus, not to your predecessor. Give them time to prove their worth to both you and the campus.

Sometime later, if they prove to be disloyal, incompetent, or not of value in their position, remove them. However, be careful not to replace them with someone already known to you because you will be accused of cronyism, he or she will never be trusted, and your reputation will suffer. To the extent possible, always fill positions with candidates who emerge during a transparent, open search.

FIVE
Dealing with Internal Constituencies

THE STUDENTS

You may have believed that when you achieved the exalted rank of president/chancellor you would no longer need to deal with the more mundane and seemingly powerless constituencies like students. But students pay your salary, ensure the financial well-being of the institution, and are the reason the university exists. So their well-being needs to be at the top of your priority list. In students' perception, the campus CEO needs to be a part of their personal experience.

Later we'll discuss indirect ways in which you influence student well-being and satisfaction, but here, we'll consider your personal interaction with students. In general, institutional leaders walk a fine line between being buddies with students and being the institutional CEO. Students, ordinarily, have no idea what a president/chancellor does. Oh, they know that person is in charge, but they have little understanding of the details of that responsibility. Assume that it is your responsibility to educate them and act accordingly at every opportunity. Some presidents/chancellors take on students as interns hoping that the interns will, in turn, inform others.

So the president/chancellor needs to help students understand his or her roles. One role is ceremonial. Your presence at commencement and other academic award ceremonies is crucial to being the campus leader. Preside over these as often as you can. Further, your presence at athletic, theater, and musical events as well as at campus-wide lectures and celebrations is important. Aside from the fact that participants deserve visible administrative support based on their own commitment and time investment, it is important to show your interest in what's occurring on campus. You can be sure that if you don't your absence will be noted.

Dealing with student government must be handled similarly. Too many campus CEOs delegate dealing with student government to the student affairs office or to somewhere else on campus. That act distances the president/chancellor from student leadership, demeans the concept of student governance, and significantly lessens the president's/chancellor's understanding of student needs. The student government officers are responsible to the students in the same way that the president/chancellor is responsible to the entire range of campus constituencies. They deserve appropriate attention, and since they are students, the campus CEO has an additional responsibility as their role model/mentor.

For many campus CEOs, being a part of their students' personal experiences does not fit the CEO's personality or value system. He or she, either by virtue of personality or personal preference, wants to remain aloof, believing that only through that behavior can he or she remain effective.

Even remaining aloof, you can still convince students that you support them if you truly do, even if you aren't willing or able to show the attitude through extensive personal interaction. Developing a belief throughout the institution that students and their well-being are top priority and ensuring that attitude is well known throughout the campus community can result from communicating the belief and making known several obvious examples of your commitment. But getting involved personally and making that involvement known in several situations is absolutely necessary.

Your goal should be for students to believe that you are working to remove every barrier to their getting an education that has nothing to do with education. This means that the campus bureaucracy, housing authority, bookstore, and student affairs division are there to serve students, providing they are committed to pursuing their academic program to the best of their abilities. If they break rules, they will be dealt with fairly. If they have personal or financial problems, they will not be subjected to a runaround or an administrative two-step. And at the same time, academic rigor, quality, and integrity will not be compromised.

Whether they know exactly what you do is not necessary, but their believing that you have their best interests at heart is. In the end, you are responsible for that perception and you must discover the way to make it happen.

THE FACULTY

Working with faculty members is as complicated, complex, and important as working with any college or university constituency. Their importance is obvious. More than any other single group, they are, as the faculty of Columbia University told Dwight David Eisenhower, "the university." And since teaching and learning are the primary business of the university, they are correct from a structural perspective. However, many faculty members take this concept to an extreme, believing that theirs is by far the most important function occurring at the university. So there is an arrogance taken on by faculty members that causes working with them to be complex.

Further, by virtue of education, training, and general intelligence, faculty members are inquisitive, creative, and analytical. When presented with data, they will dissect it. When presented with issues unsupported by data, they will fill in the blanks, correctly or incorrectly. When difficult situations arise on campus, lacking facts, they will create scenarios and pass them on as rumors. So dealing with faculty members, in general, requires honesty, transparency, and a willingness to share data far beyond what might normally be expected outside of academia.

Also required is a willingness to be available to them so that they can discover the facts on their own. So while dishonesty or withholding information may well lead to faculty disrespect, the same can occur if you are invisible or unavailable.

At the same time that faculty members must be respected for their intelligence, it is important that you quickly establish that theirs is not the only voice to be heard on campus. Other constituencies have rights and responsibilities, and both their jobs and sensitivities are worthy of note. Ensure that every employee on campus believes that he or she has an important job, and even though some get paid more than others or have more responsibility, all have a role to play in the ultimate responsibility of the campus and the education and welfare of students. Where faculty members are concerned, the realization that they are not the only constituency on campus can go a long way toward easing tensions when problems arise.

Structural issues also complicate interactions with faculty members. Most academic institutions are divided into departments, colleges, and/or schools and sometimes divisions under the general umbrella of academic affairs. And while individual faculty members are guided and driven by their own backgrounds and personalities, departments, schools and colleges, and divisions also have personalities, which lead to unique reactions to issues and adversities. So in his or her dealings, the president/chancellor must account for these idiosyncratic behaviors.

Further complicating the interaction with faculty members are conceptual and other structural issues. Academic institutions function based on the concept of shared governance. The faculty members exercise the lion's share through an organization most often called the academic senate. It is usually the senate to which administrators go when consulting on issues and it is the senate that promulgates policy suggestions on behalf of the faculty to the administration.

So to deal with faculty members the president/chancellor must navigate individual faculty personalities, department and school/college idiosyncrasies, and senate wants and needs. Overlaying all of this structure are concepts of academic freedom, faculty rights and responsibilities, freedom of speech, academic prerogatives, and faculty control of curriculum.

CAMPUS COMMITTEES AND TASK FORCES

The promise of campus committees is that of cooperative decision making, shared governance, and collaborative behavior in general. The danger of such committees is the prospect of loss of control and the damage possible to the president's/chancellor's reputation resulting from his or her attendance (or lack of same) or behavior.

The spectrum of committees on which a campus leader is expected to serve or lead depends on the individual campus. On some, the CEO is expected to attend or even lead the senate. On others, the presence of the campus leader is deemed intrusive. On many campuses, participation on diversity committees, strategic planning committees, and emergency management committees, and in meetings with faculty and staff leadership, and more, is expected.

Participation on committees gives you a means to be visible, dispel rumors, correct information, and participate in that part of campus life. It is important that the campus community sees you as involved.

Task forces are a slightly different animal. They are, ordinarily, groups focused on a specific, complex task. They usually have a specific goal like formulation of a strategic plan that justifies their existence. And they are usually chartered by the president or chancellor. These are group efforts in which you cannot afford not to participate! Too many negatives? Your presence on these task forces is required. Their importance is clear by virtue of your having chartered them. So not participating would be noticed and condemned.

Most important in all of this discussion is that you take advantage of the aspects of committee participation. Done right, participating can only enhance your tenure.

Behavior with Committees

Several pieces of advice concerning participation might be helpful.

1. When chairing any committee, don't talk too much or pontificate. Often, such behavior is seen as attempting to take over or bully the committee. You already run the campus, so there's no real point in assuming control of a committee that probably advises you.

2. As a committee member, don't talk too much or pontificate, for all of the reasons cited in 1.
3. When another committee member presents erroneous information, respond only if correcting the error is critical. Being a know-it-all is not a reputation worth coveting.
4. If an error of yours is pointed out, be gracious in your response.
5. Make humorous comments only if you're sure of your audience.
6. Carry your weight when the committee has work to do.
7. Don't miss meetings except for the best of reasons and make those reasons known. Missing meetings will give the impression that you don't care about the issues and, by extension, the campus.

DIRECT REPORTS AND OTHER STAFF

Your interaction with those who report directly to you is determined by their function within the organization. If direct reports are simply convenient targets when things go wrong and you need someone to blame while you take credit for what goes right, then your interaction will probably comprise a set of arm's-length behaviors. And each time you blame one of them or take credit that others deserve, their respect for you will wane. However, some organizations seem to function well in this sort of toxic environment.

However, if the function of direct reports is to take responsibility for the nurturing and growth of their part of the institution, then the interactions take on a far different character. The requirement for your behavior is for support and accountability. It's a lot like the Reagan-era expression, "trust but verify." Supporting your direct reports includes respecting their ideas, providing advice and resources to achieve agreed-on goals, and making your support of them obvious throughout the organization. It also includes buffering them from forces and individuals external to their organizations (boards, legislators, donors) who would influence their decisions for purposes other than those of the institution.

Further, in instances where direct reports are the target of complaint or criticism, it is important that you gather as much information as possible (listen to both sides of the story) before making a final judgment. Your aim is fairness in support of institutional goals. However, whatever the final outcome, it is important that your initial position is in support of your subordinate. (Trust but verify.)

Finally, don't try to take credit for what your people do. Nothing short of dishonesty and criminal behavior will more quickly decrease their respect for you.

Loyalty

Loyalty is a two-way street! Your colleagues and subordinates will express and act out loyalty to you only if you behave similarly toward them. It's a simple concept, but one that is misunderstood and ignored by leaders. And they ignore it at their peril.

When a president/chancellor assumes his or her position, he or she must decide whether direct reports and other staff will remain in their positions or be separated, transferred, or demoted. Some leaders will prudently decide to wait and assess performance before making any such decisions. Others will act immediately.

For those who act immediately, to the extent possible, explain any separations in terms of your loyalty to the institution and act in a humane manner. Failing to do so will immediately make suspect your loyalty to employees. In rare cases, the separated, transferred, or demoted employee will have been widely judged incompetent or otherwise unworthy, but even in the best of these situations, it is your reputation that is on the line. How you behave will be the subject of multiple campus discussions.

As you begin to interact on campus, situations will emerge where faculty and staff make minor mistakes, transgress in one way or another, or behave in manners contrary to campus values. When this happens and you are involved, your behavior and response should be restorative and rehabilitative. Your reputation as a leader will suffer massively if you respond by berating the employee or meting out some sort of punishment. You will be seen as disloyal to faculty and staff and only concerned with your own needs.

Where illegal, destructive, or otherwise egregious behavior occurs, your reaction must be seen as just and appropriate. This is another test of loyalty. Even if your reaction is intense and the consequences to the employee are life altering, you can emerge as loyal to the institution and loyal to and supportive of those who toil there. After all, you are protecting the integrity of the institution and the well-being of those who work there.

Similarly, if there are external threats to the institution, visible defense will be another measure of your loyalty to both the institution and the faculty and staff. When budgets are cut externally, the institution is accused of supporting liberal causes, relationships with the community sour, or the ideas of individual faculty are attacked in the press, that's the time to stand up and earn the loyalty of your colleagues and staff. It is important for them to feel that you have their backs.

When students or staff members express dissatisfaction with an employee's or student's behavior, offer to investigate the situation. Do not allow yourself to be infected with their outrage or immediately take their side. Where accusations against employees and students are concerned, assume their proper behavior, but verify. This is another example of your showing loyalty.

Your behavior will be repaid in kind. If faculty and staff believe that you are loyal to them, they will behave loyally toward you. They will speak glowingly of you and the institution in the community, discount rumors and gossip and not spread unverified stories, and listen carefully to your proposals and ideas.

However, don't expect them to lie for you or otherwise engage in unethical behavior on your behalf.

THE CAMPUS POLICE FORCE

Campus security can be structured in a number of ways. The force can consist of sworn officers who have the same authorities and powers granted to local law enforcement including that of carrying weapons. The force might comprise sworn officers who do not carry weapons. Campus security might even be the responsibility of a private security contractor hired by the institution.

Whatever the arrangement, the president/chancellor should develop a close relationship with them so that they readily share information with him or her about conditions on campus, sensitive situations, and indications of illegal activity on the campus. In addition, because any institution of higher education needs to maintain a collaborative, supportive environment, the police force should adopt a "community policing" approach wherein the force promotes partnerships and programs that promote public safety in collaboration with the campus community rather than simply chasing down, tackling, and arresting those behaving illegally.

In addition it is important to promote collaboration with local law enforcement to ensure that local conditions surrounding the campus do not cause deterioration of the campus environment. The collaboration must be reciprocal, and local law enforcement should feel that it is being supported as well.

Cops and Robbers and Students

Maintaining the balance between ensuring the security of the campus environment and fostering an open, nonrepressive campus atmosphere is delicate and difficult. On one hand, the perception that anything goes on campus or the presence of illegal activity or a belief that campus security is lax will be detrimental to institutional reputation, community relations, and parental confidence. On the other, an aggressive police force, the use of metal detectors at the entrances to campus events, and shotguns and assault weapons being openly carried in police vehicles send a negative message about campus safety, personal expression, and the open exchange of ideas.

It is possible to find the balance by encouraging community policing, open communication between law enforcement officers and constituents, common sense, and prudent risk management. Community policing requires that the entire campus community embrace the idea that campus security is everyone's responsibility and that community vigilance and collaboration will ensure campus safety. And the approach will succeed only if there is open communication between law enforcement and constituents.

It is also important that common sense prevail. Every unusual behavior is not a threat. Every touch is not a malicious assault. Every introvert is not a serial killer waiting to pounce. While it is appropriate to err on the side of caution, it is inappropriate to serially overreact.

And that thought leads to prudent risk management. It is a giant intellectual leap from helping the campus to be aware of safety and security incidents to enforcing a solution for every negative campus incident. Banning all fraternity parties or considering removal of all fraternities from campus because one fraternity transgresses is one example of imprudent risk management. Opening stairwells to only emergency use because an incident occurs in a stairwell is another. Employing metal detectors and purse searches claiming security issues when the reason for the action is an athletic director who wants greater concession revenue is a third and egregious misuse of risk management.

Several suggestions for hiring security personnel might be useful:

1. Employ a force of sworn officers. Their training and authority will serve the institution well.
2. For leadership positions, promote and hire only personnel who have had experience on a campus.
3. Ensure that there is diverse depth of experience among the force. Longer-serving officers may calm the aggressive approach of newer officers.
4. Don't hesitate to hire second-career officers from community forces. Their experience will serve the institution well.
5. Ensure that officer training is continual and adequately funded.

LAWYERS

Lawyers come in two flavors, those who are "fer ya" and those who are "agin ya" (or those who represent the institution and those who represent the opposition). The statement is an oversimplification and an exaggeration at the same time. It is an exaggeration because lawyers are trained to analyze complicated cases where they may have little disciplinary expertise and to present coherent, compelling arguments as representatives of an institution or individual. In that way, they are all alike. And they deserve respect because they must be continual learners and quickly become experts in disciplines where they were not trained.

It is an oversimplification because lawyers ply their trade in many ways and not all legal interactions are adversarial. As the president/chancellor you must be aware of a spectrum of possibilities.

Initially, it is important to understand whom legal counsel represents. In higher education, legal counsel represents the institution and the board, which is responsible for the institution. It does not represent individual board members or you, except when institutional and individual interests are congruent. That's why you need to retain your own legal counsel in contract negotiations with the board.

Adversarial issues present an important legal challenge. On one side of any issue is your legal support. Legal support to the institution can be provided in several forms. The institution may hire in-house counsel, retain a group of attorneys in private practice, or use a combination of the two approaches. Each has advantages and disadvantages.

Advantages of in-house counsel include knowledge of institutional history, focus on institutional issues and development of special expertise in education law, and loyalty based on employment. Disadvantages include absence of advisory backup and research capabilities available in large legal practices and loss of the competitive edge and intensity that private practice requires. Some of the issues of research and expertise can be ameliorated if the institution includes a law school that is willing to collaborate. However, such arrangements can also lead to destructive conflicts of interest.

Retaining external counsel can improve backup and intensity. But focus on the institution dissipates, and knowledge of institutional history, tradition, and practice can be sparse. Additionally, care must be taken to ensure that development of an income stream does not take precedence over institutional needs and priorities.

A compromise organizational solution includes hiring an internal legal adviser who is responsible for retaining external counsel to deal with specific issues. In this way, the sense of loyalty to the institution is retained, and the legal adviser can provide oversight functions knowledgeably.

On the other side of adversarial issues are lawyers who represent aggrieved parties or opponents of the university. These are usually attorneys in private practice whose remuneration and reputation may depend on their winning, and they act accordingly. If they are part of a large firm, they can depend on a research staff and the advice of colleagues. If they are in solo or small practices, their resources are much more limited.

It is in your best interest for you and your legal support to know the opposition to assess the challenge. It is also in your interest to become acquainted with members of the local legal community because, often, grievances can be worked out to mutual satisfaction before they are injected into the civil system.

It is important to realize that when lawyers are involved, issues, whether adversarial or not, are often extremely complicated mixtures of personal interests, institutional interests, legal considerations, and ethical judgments. Your lawyers are only advisers. It is important for you, as the leader, to take the time to understand the detail and draw independent conclusions on which to base your decisions.

Tips for Dealing with Lawyers

Interacting with the legal profession can be tricky and complicated. A few pieces of advice might be helpful:

1. Your lawyers work for you and the institution. Don't let them make your decisions.
2. When attempting to solve a problem, do not ask legal counsel whether a solution can be executed; ask how it can be done. Do not accept any solution that is unethical or illegal.
3. Once a case has been filed, never speak to opposing counsel when your counsel is not present.
4. Do not trust opposing counsel's statements. Verify before responding.
5. In discussion and negotiation, let your legal counsel speak for you. Protect your position as decision maker.
6. If your counsel proclaims the strength of your case in its early stages and then equivocates and advocates settling as the trial date approaches, be suspicious. It may be that some new and damaging evidence has appeared, but it is more likely that the lawyer is not up to the task or is inflating his or her fees.
7. When hiring external counsel, shop around and use price, specific expertise, and reputation as your criteria.

THE SENATE

Senates can be more or less powerful depending on the institution, their charter and bylaws, and the circumstance in which they find themselves. Some senates represent the entire university faculty and staff. Some represent only the faculty. Staff members are represented by other organizations. Some even have student representatives. Senates can have charters that grant them broad decisional powers, or they may have only advisory authority. But wherever they fall in the spectrum of authority, they provide a bully pulpit from which faculty and/or staff can make their opinions known to the media, campus, and general public.

The senate must, therefore, be dealt with in an honest, straightforward manner. Nothing undermines the credibility and authority of a president/chancellor more than being caught in a public lie or appearing to obfuscate on important issues during senate deliberations. Of course, appearing to be weak and indecisive has its pitfalls, but those are personality weaknesses, not willfully negative behaviors.

The authorities possible for a senate are also massively dependent on whether the campus is subject to faculty collective bargaining. Collective bargaining agents retain authority over salaries, wages, and conditions of employment as well as the grievance procedures related to them. In those situations, the senate often retains input only into curricular and other academic issues.

Even more interesting is that in some senates, the constituents elect a presiding officer from among their ranks. In other cases, you as president/chancellor are the presiding and convening officer. This arrangement affords you a most influential position but also a most visible and vulnerable position. Care must be exercised in every interaction with the body.

In still others, the senate meets in the absence of any institutional executive. This situation, of course, affords you the least influence but allows you to distance yourself from their decisions. Yet you want their advice and decisions to be as informed and useful as possible, so your central responsibility becomes providing accurate, adequate information for their processes.

When the CEO is involved in senate deliberations, care must be taken to provide exactly the right amount of input. If you speak too much, you may be accused of meddling, interfering, or micromanaging. If you speak too little, you will be accused of being distant, aloof, and unwilling to accept input. In most cases, the following are good rules of thumb:

1. Answer quickly and directly when asked direct questions.
2. Correct misinformation gently, but quickly, when it comes to light.
3. Enter into debates extremely sparingly, even when your honor is in question.
4. Always remain civil and refrain from ad hominem statements. They result in your appearing to be petty and mean.

In general, lead when necessary. Otherwise, let others in the body do your work for you.

And in that regard, meet regularly with faculty leaders (presiding officer and standing committee chairs) to inform them, let them know who you are, and solicit their help in moving the institution in the direction you envision for it.

Academic Freedom

Academic freedom is the most protected and abused of university faculty rights. Often partially confused with freedom of speech, it gives faculty members protection when they choose to research, express opinions concerning, and teach about subjects that are controversial. However, as interpreted in the United States, the protection applies only to subject matter within a faculty member's expertise. So a physicist commenting on right to life in the classroom does not fall within the purview of academic freedom, nor does a professor of English literature commenting on the scientific quality of a physics professor's publications.

Such offerings are protected under the first amendment from government sanction, but they may cause a reaction under the aegis of university civility rules or as the result of personal response by individuals on the campus. Freedom of speech allows such utterances, but that freedom may not come without consequences.

In similar fashion, university students are protected under the academic freedom umbrella. If a student as part of his or her curriculum participates in controversial behavior, the university is obligated to protect him or her. The most common examples occur in visual and performing arts programs. Depictions of controversial materials such as nudity, sexual behavior, racial bias, graphic violence, and confrontation to organized religious will almost always elicit constituency reactions contrary to what the university believes are faculty and institutional prerogatives.

This is also true of theater productions that confront accepted community norms and standards. In all of these circumstances, the university is expected to zealously guard the integrity of the institution and its commitment to academic freedom.

There are, however, campus situations where academic freedom is not an applicable concept or protected. When faculty members decide to criticize each other uncivilly, it is unclear whether the actions are protected. Hate speech is clearly unprotected. And while it could be argued that university management is an area of faculty members' expertise and they have every right to teach about it, research it, and speak about it, discussing university issues in unrelated classes may not be covered by academic freedom. On the other hand, speaking in an academic senate is protected by practice and tradition.

Unfortunately, most faculty members will claim the protection of academic freedom with respect to any utterance they might make. Within that claim lies the abuse. Academic freedom is a fairly specific doctrine and simply does not apply broadly to just any faculty utterance. Thus, faculty should be extremely careful when claiming that protection.

However, presidents/chancellors must be similarly cautious when assuming that academic freedom does not apply to a specific faculty or student behavior. The concept is so universally misunderstood that even when it doesn't apply, faculty will stand together in opposition to anyone attempting to sanction the involved faculty member or members. So a president/chancellor, even in the most obvious situations, contradicts the invocation of academic freedom at his or her peril. In any event, it is best to attempt to solve such situations in less direct ways rather than risk sanction by your own faculty, the American Association of University Professors, AAUP; notoriously intolerant in most situations, or any of the institution's other constituencies.

The best advice is be careful!

SIX

The Board

Trustees, Visitors, and Otherwise

For any CEO, the board members (whether they are called visitors, trustees, advisers, rectors, or whatever) of the institution are among the most important of your constituencies. After all, if the board is properly executing its responsibilities, it hires or fires you, holds you responsible for the success or failure of the institution, and approves policy governing institutional operation. So your relationship with the board members is integral to your continuation and success as president/chancellor.

With that in mind, first, consider why individual board members are serving. For some, there exists a genuine belief in and loyalty to the institution. Service on the board is an important obligation. For others, being named to the board serves their ego and enhances their résumé. For still others, it is an elected position or political appointment that is a stepping-stone to bigger things. Some have been convinced to serve by others for one reason or another and really don't care. And for a few, it is a means to regaining their youth, reliving their college and/or fraternity experiences, and going home again . . . much akin to buying a sporty convertible at midlife. For most, it is some combination of all of these reasons. But in interacting with boards, it is important to identify which of these motivations is overriding for each member.

The reasoning is obvious. For board members who are primarily interested in what's best for the university, communicating well and often, presenting information (challenges and solutions) in a straightforward, logical manner, and requesting policy promulgation using arguments based on institutional improvement is probably sufficient to achieve your ends. For those whose primary focus is political and or personal, the same general guidelines apply, but also taken into account must be the opinions of the political constituencies of those board members. For those who don't care, it doesn't matter how issues are presented as long as you don't personally insult or confront them. And for those who are simply reliving their earlier experiences, taking them drinking and to athletic events will get you as far as any other behavior. However, the bottom line is that board members must be cultivated similarly to donors or legislators, and account must be taken of their individual characteristics.

Another aspect of board interaction is board size. Large boards can be difficult to manage due to the multiplicity of agendas present, but they often have more members who are less engaged and as a whole seldom are of one mind on issues. Thus, they can be more easily led toward a desired outcome. However, they are least likely to support you in difficult situations. Small boards are more easily swayed by one member's biases, and they tend to micromanage but have fewer members who need to be convinced to think like you. Thus, they are more likely to support you in difficult situations but might, on their own, decide that you are the cause of the difficulty.

If one of the functions of the board is to provide financial support when shortfalls occur (as is often the case in private institutions), having more people of wealth on the board is positive. When attempting to convince the board to move in a specific direction or to make a difficult decision, having fewer members is better.

To what end are boards cultivated? Your goal should be to focus the board on their primary functions—evaluating you and the health of the institution and approving policy in that regard. While they need to understand institutional functions in excruciating detail, that should not tempt them to meddle in the management of the institution. By holding you responsible for the success or failure of the institution, they allow you to fully accept that responsibility and give you help and support when asked. Remember that you lead and manage; they oversee.

The governing board may not be the only one with which you must deal. The university may have a foundation board, an alumni board, and numerous advisory boards. The principles for dealing with them remain the same. Honest, open, and fulsome communications are your best vehicles for dealing with these boards, but individual board member idiosyncrasies must be accounted for. Keep in mind that while the governing board may have the charted authority to hire and fire you, these boards may be equally powerful and may require similar attention and respect.

BOARD BEHAVIORS

The character and personality of any board is determined by that of the individual board members and the board chair. In general, board members who are alumni will feel some loyalty to the institution. Board members who have been CEOs in the private sector will attempt to second-guess you and manage the institution. And board members who were academics will believe that they know much more about the subtleties of academia than you do.

But you get the picture. Board members are usually successful, self-assured professionals who believe they understand organizations. Few have led an organization as complicated as yours, and few have had to satisfy as many constituencies. It's your job to educate them to gain enough operating space to do your job.

That education begins as you carefully monitor your own behavior. In presentations to the board, never present problems without suggesting solutions. If you need advice, find it elsewhere or ask trusted members individually. They are not an advisory board.

When you are presenting requests for policy approval, accept small changes gracefully. Any policy can be made clearer and better. However, if major changes are suggested, request that the policy be returned to the staff for further deliberation. The board should be approving policy that you have carefully crafted, not making policy.

When individual board members suggest hiring specific people to fill vacancies or suggest creating positions to employ friends or relatives, deflect to the extent prudent. Assess the situation to decide whether the possibility of losing or gaining a supporter on the board is worth the risk of questionable behavior. In some instances, you can ask the board chair to intervene.

Similarly, when asked to accommodate individual board members using institutional resources, while it may be appropriate in some cases, fulfilling the request may be illegal or contrary to institutional policy in others. Assess the risk and act accordingly.

In most situations, it is best not to develop close relationships with individual board members. Such interactions can have unintended consequences. Imagine:

1. The board chair who spends several hours one evening each week on the phone with the president/chancellor outlining the work for the week.
2. The farm-owning board member who insists that the agriculture program provide him with technical support and crop futures knowledge.
3. The ambitious board member who asks for student help and faculty expertise in support of his or her political aspirations.
4. The board member who uses institutional transportation to transport family and friends.
5. The board member who entertains business clients at institutional expense.

Despite their egregious nature, these situations are not only possible but have occurred.

To be sure, most board members would not consider engaging in such questionable practices, and many have only the well-being of the institution and the students at heart. But boards can bring tremendous pressure to bear on the president/chancellor, and the few members who transgress can sorely test the president's/chancellor's values and standards.

SEVEN
Dealing with External Constituencies

DONORS AND OTHER UNIVERSITY FRIENDS

Donors are more or less financially important to an institution, depending on the percentage of the institutional budget for which their contributions are responsible. However, emotionally and in terms of university self- and external image, their presence and attitudes are critical for all institutions.

Financially, it has been the tradition that donors have contributed larger sums (as a percentage of budgets) to private institutions than to public institutions, but that tradition is changing as state financial support for public institutions has decreased. So fund-raising, donor relations, and the development office must be bright on an institutional CEO's radar screen.

So whether the institution has a well-oiled development operation and the chief development office is highly effective, it falls to the president/chancellor as the face of the institution to be the primary development officer, partner in cultivation, and closer of deals. Put simply, the campus CEO must be the development role model.

And the president/chancellor should realize that in support of development, everyone in the institution must be involved because it is just as probable that a donor might feel warmly toward the institution as the result of interaction with a single faculty or staff member as it is that a donor can be put off by the behavior of the president/chancellor. Everyone is responsible for the success or failure of a development program.

Let's begin with major gifts. Getting started in development of major gifts requires an understanding of why people give. Some donors give in support of scholarships because they have genuine affection for students and the institution. Some give to brick and mortar projects because having their name lastingly affixed to a building gives them a feeling of immortality. Some give to specific projects because they have an abiding belief in the project's goals. Some give to satisfy their feeling of obligation for the institution. Some give because they want the football team to win. And some simply have a tax problem and need the relief that comes from giving. But for whatever reasons a donor gives, it is the responsibility of the development office and/or the president/chancellor to ferret out those reasons and honor them.

A second tenet of major gifts development is communicating a clear institutional message that is carried forward by all involved with the process. When a donor is visited multiple times by different representatives of the university, it is counterproductive for one to identify scholarships as the highest priority for gifts and another to ask for funds to start a program or to build buildings. The message must be clear and consistent, or the donor will not trust the institution to use his or her money wisely. In fact, the donor might even reach the conclusion that the university will not use the gift in keeping with the donor's intent, if the institutional representatives give the wrong impression.

A third aspect of a major gifts development program is the need to ensure that the overall program supports as many constituencies within the institution as possible. A program can be severely crippled if one area of the university believes that donations are flowing to satisfy only one university priority. Most commonly, this phenomenon occurs where fund-raising for athletics is prominent and that for other programs receives much less attention. In those cases, the possibility that people in other programs will sabotage athletics development by making public their discontent is very real.

Successful development programs also require patience and persistence. Donors will give according to their own time table, and no amount of pushing, prodding, begging, cajoling, or wheedling will cause them to give at any other than the time of their choice. Just keep at it. Some donors will, quite simply, be suspicious of your motives and want to wait to ensure you're the upstanding representative of the institution that you say you are. So cultivation takes time. It takes time to develop donor trust and create and explain the programs for which you are soliciting support, and for donors to decide. So if you're impatient by nature, put a cork in it or let others do the cultivation work.

But at the same time, realize that it is the campus CEO who has the responsibility for making the final deal. Most donors will deal only with you, so be prepared and available.

Another program related to major gifts is bequests. Some donors rely on an almost religious belief that they can't give up any of their wealth until they die. While there is some logic to the fear that you might run out of money before you die, it is often an irrational fear, but needs to be respected by development personnel. Trust is, once again, central to governing bequests. Donors must believe that their funds will be used in accordance with their wishes and specifications. Again, building such trust takes time and patience is, once again, a virtue.

Finally, annual funds—collections of small gifts requested annually— are usually organized by the development office and do not involve you except for a small number of group appearances and gifts. In this case, let them do their job and don't meddle.

Advice for Interacting with Donors

Donations from private sources are not only important because of their intrinsic value to the university but also in improving the institution's self-image and its reputation. After all, if donors are willing to contribute parts of their personal wealth to an organization, it must be a deserving entity.

However, donors can be sensitive, fickle, demanding, and altogether difficult to deal with, as can universities. Imagine several situations where donors and the institution can have difficulty:

1. A donor offers a substantial sum of construction money to a university with the understanding that the certain design conditions for the building will be met and parts of the building will be named for him or her. After the deal has been accepted, the donor insists on changing the design conditions, causing the university to negate the deal and return the funds, earning the donor's undying enmity.
2. A donor contacts the university about providing a major gift and attends several dinners and events hosted by the university before declaring that he or she is not interested.
3. A university accepts a substantial gift meant to endow scholarships for talented students. Sometime later, the donor discovers that the university established the endowment but is awarding the scholarships based on need, not academic accomplishment.
4. A university solicits and accepts gifts in support of an athletic endowment and uses the money to support ongoing athletic operations.
5. An academic department solicits private funds to purchase a costly item of scientific equipment. Subsequently, the department applies for and receives federal funds to purchase the item and uses the donated funds for other purposes. The donor is never informed but finds out later from another source.

These situations are examples of major gaffs and fundamental dishonesty that can degrade the effectiveness of development operations and cause loss of future gifts. However, many seemingly minor transgressions can also cause problems. A couple of tips might help to avoid such issues:

1. Whether the institution employs a chief development officer, you are the chief development officer and the face of the university. Donors, especially major ones, will expect to deal with you.
2. When arranging a meeting with an individual donor, be clear about the purpose of the meeting. Whether the meeting's purpose is to request specific support, inform the donor about the institution, or get better acquainted, knowing what to expect will relieve pressure and better ensure a successful exchange. If the stated purpose is to request funds and the donor refuses the meeting, you have saved yourself some time.
3. Invest energy in learning about the donor—his or her interests and background. The donor will appreciate your interest.
4. Remember the names of donors and recognize them when you happen to meet them. Calling a person by the wrong name or not recognizing him or her at all is a quick way to lose support.
5. Requesting nonspecific support will be unsuccessful with most potential donors. Project-based requests carry a much greater probability of success because donors identify with buildings, scholarships, scientific equipment, and child-care centers, among other possibilities.
6. If your alumni base is small or the percentage of alumni who donate is not large, be patient and allow your development professionals to build the base.
7. Utilize current donors to help recruit and cultivate potential donors.

Patience is your greatest ally in the development arena. Moving too quickly or too aggressively will increase the probability of failure.

THE LEGISLATURE AND OTHER GOVERNMENT OFFICIALS AND GOVERNMENT AGENCIES

For presidents/chancellors of public institutions, dealing productively with elected (and appointed) government officials is central to financial support of the institution. And while state government officials are more central to the financial well-being of a public institution, local and federal officials can help, but they are more effective in enhancing the image and external relationships necessary to the institution than in helping financially.

Private institutions are not as dependent on government officials for direct financial support, yet those same officials can be critical to engendering positive local attitudes, decreasing red tape and bureaucracy in official processes, and generally ensuring that few barriers to institutional goals exist. So developing positive relationships with government officials is necessary, no matter which institutional type you serve.

Dealing with the staffs of elected officials can be incredibly frustrating. Often, the staffs of elected officials are chosen because they have worked on the successful election campaign of the official. But that qualification gives them no special ability to do their job. So having been in higher education for decades and being passionate about an issue that you have worked on for many years can lead to irritation when trying to convince a twenty-something staffer who knows nothing about the subject that his or her elected official boss should give you audience and care about the issue as much as you do.

And the arrogance that many staffers exhibit will do nothing but raise your blood pressure. While your patience may be sorely tested, remain calm, rely on your belief in the issue, and be persistent. However, you can lessen the severity of dealing with this sort of problem by finding the most experienced staffer and dealing with him or her.

Dealing with government agencies often requires dealing with multiple elected and/or appointed officials. Those near the bottom of the hierarchy will ordinarily slavishly follow the rules and be unable to deal with issues that are ambiguous or nonstandard. So when dealing with an agency, interact with the highest-ranking accessible official.

Whatever the situation, remember that elected officials (and to a certain extent appointed ones) have achieved success through interaction with voters. Make your interaction with elected officials personal! Eat with them, play golf with them, or contribute to their campaigns by playing poker with them. In an extreme case, you might even attend an opera or professional wrestling. The point is, it's harder to turn down a friend who asks for a favor or help than it is to turn down an acquaintance.

Dealing with Public Officials

Here are some observations, suggestions, and rules of thumb in dealing with government officials:

1. Accept the fact that, effectively, elected officials are responsible to no one. Certainly, they are responsible to their voting constituency once every two, four, or six years, but those time frames are long and memories are short. Unless they have great strength of character and clear view of right from wrong, their treatment of you and your institution will depend on your ability to cultivate their friendship.
2. Appointed officials are responsible to their appointing authority. Cultivation of individuals and their appointing authority are equally important.

3. Bartering is a way of life among government officials. When asked for a favor, unless it is illegal or immoral or scandalous, try your best to grant it. However, also make sure that whatever you do won't embarrass you if it's reported in the press.
4. To the best of your ability, try not to meet with government officials (especially elected ones) alone. Take a colleague along. Do this not only because it is prudent to have a witness to whatever is agreed on but also to be better able to explain any point you are making. Additionally, your points are probably complex enough that further explanations are necessary, and colleagues are more often able to observe misunderstandings and their roots while you are talking.
5. Keep in mind that elections are not won on the strength of candidates' expertise in any field, so most elected officials will not know much about educational institutions. Your problems begin when elected officials believe they know about education because they believe they have gotten one. Nothing is more dangerous to achieving your goals than officials who are misinformed or acting on inaccurate beliefs. Do your best to inform them when dealing with any issue, and only after that try to bias their views one way or another. Appointed officials often have expertise that qualifies them for their appointed post. However, that is not always the case. Some may have been appointed solely on the basis of friendship or obligation and know little about their fields. Informing them may be as important as informing elected officials.
6. Elected officials often hold fund-raisers. Remain aloof from them, unless you're invited to theirs and their opponents' without contribution. Contributing gets your name on public lists. If the opponent wins the election, you have dug a hole that is difficult to escape, and there is little chance that any level of cultivation will regain the confidence of the aggrieved party. Even if you contribute equally to both sides, one or the other may take offense.
7. Be careful to follow the rules for interaction with government officials. Certainly there are federal and state rules concerning gifts and invitations to events, but there are often institutional rules as well. Your credibility and integrity are damaged when it becomes known that breaches have occurred. Even worse, your tenure can be cut short if the breach is deemed sufficiently egregious.
8. Make an effort to talk to officials even when there is no issue. Most officials, especially legislators, resent being contacted only when you want special consideration or specific relief.

THE PRESS, MEDIA, AND OTHER PUBLIC GROUPS

Many presidents/chancellors of educational institutions expend vast amounts of energy avoiding the press and concocting means to spin any news that is remotely negative. But much less energy is required to develop a positive working relationship with the press, and spinning news eventually results in public distrust. Reporters, editors, and publishers respond well to direct communication and respect for their need to succeed at their job. Few are out to get you or your institution, and if they are, it is relatively easy to identify and avoid or confront their issues.

Developing a positive media relationship has many advantages. Aside from the effect on the image of your institution (and you), reporters will often inform you about campus situations or breaking news stories before your staff informs you. That allows you to comment on and get out in front of the issue. Also, you will have no shortage of on-campus and off-campus individuals whose goals are reached by having a negative light cast on the institution. To accomplish that, they will call media and plant stories, whether true or false. Friendly reporters will often short-circuit such efforts, or at least inform you that they are occurring.

Dealing with television news people requires similar attention. But they work on shorter timelines. Developing relationships with them is slightly more difficult since the encounters are fleeting. However, when you encounter them in situations where their story doesn't center on you or your institution, engage them in conversation, show interest in their work, learn their names, and help them become comfortable with you. This advice is especially important in dealing with the people who wield the video cameras. Often, they are the interviewers, and their approach to a story can make you a hero or a heel. The investment of time will pay off later.

All of these suggestions need to be placed in context. No matter how carefully you manage an institution or you interact, there are bound to be situations that result in negative publicity. Unless the story concerns major institutional scandal or you are accused of criminal or immoral behavior, the spotlight will quickly move to another issue. Television news has about a two-day run before interest disappears, and newspapers are widely unread beyond their headlines. In fact, as circulation of newspapers decreases, one wonders whether even the headlines are read. Don't overreact or overdefend.

The greatest danger to you or your institution is having a reporter continually dwell on negative stories. Only continual negativity will have a lasting effect. So unless you have raised the ire of a reporter to the extent that he or she is out to get you, expend your energy developing positive media relationships and ensuring that as much general information about the university as possible is publicized.

Developing a Relationship with Reporters and Editors

Here are a few tips for cultivating press and media relationships:

1. When reporters call for information, make yourself available. Don't respond only through university spokespeople. The behavior dehumanizes you and makes it easier for the reporter to see the dark side of any story.
2. Respond quickly to queries. Reporters are controlled by deadlines and appreciative of not being given a slow roll.
3. Respond to questions directly. Don't tell long stories or talk around an issue. Such behavior increases suspicion that the real story is being hidden.
4. Take advantage of every opportunity to speak to reporters off the record. Such conversation gives them background information, makes their work easier, and develops your working relationship with them.
5. Plan to speak regularly with editorial boards of newspapers and magazines. They are interested in what you're doing and they influence reporters. Of course, they also write opinion pieces and those are critical to public opinion of you and your institution.
6. Don't lie. Getting caught in a lie permanently damages your relationship with most news people. Post lying, no matter how professional they are, they will always color their stories when you're involved.

ALUMNI

Alumni as a group own the most complete and in-depth corporate memory of institutional environment of any of a president's/chancellor's constituents. After all, from deep inside, they have seen the institution's workings. And they have personally experienced the individual changes that result from the institution's pursuing its mission. They can be the most positive public relations tool of a college or university, or they can have a most devastating effect on the institution's reputation.

So the institutional leader's first responsibility to alumni occurs during their student years. Their experiences as students shape their attitudes as alumni. Then after graduation, the continuing responsibility to alumni is to remind them of the value and quality of their earlier experiences to engender future loyalty and convince them of the institution's continuing value to them. It is their feelings about the college or university that will cause them to be donors, recruiters, and cheerleaders for the institution.

Developing productive interactions with alumni is not rocket science. Reminding them of their memorable and good experiences as students, treating them well when they have contact with the institution, and providing services that reinforce their belief in the importance of the institution to them personally are the basics. And that means staffing an alumni office with people who are of positive mind and attitude toward the institution and believe in treating customers well, because alumni are, in fact, the customers.

Contact and communication are of great importance, and the institution must balance the use of old-school mailing and telephone contacts with modern social networking technologies.

Structural issues surrounding an alumni organization are slightly more complicated. Ordinarily, alumni organizations are of two types, internal to the institution or independent of the institution. Choice of one or the other often depends on institutional size, institutional goals for the organization, and whether an institution is public or private. Several examples are useful.

If the organization is internal to the institution, it is governed by applicable institutional policies. Public institutions are subject to state rules and regulations. And for very large public institutions, the broad spectrum of activities in which an alumni office is officially engaged can present massive challenges to those rules. So separating the alumni organization from the institution can be prudent.

However, the loss of institutional control of the alumni organization can be challenging. To be sure, institutional officials serving on the board can restore some control, but the organization is fundamentally independent. Thus, imagine the difficulty if the university makes a decision that is negative for, say, athletics and the independent alumni organization publicly disagrees. The consequences for the institution and for fundraising, reputation, and external relations can be devastating.

Private institutions (free from suffering the governmental control of public institutions) most often include their alumni functions within the institution to enhance the development function. However, very large, private institutions may choose to separate the organizations entirely.

In contrast, integrating alumni organizations (internal or independent) into campus activities has many positives. Having current students and alumni interact and current faculty and staff interact with alumni, and hosting community events at which alumni and community friends interact can be helpful not only in improving relationships among the groups but also in helping faculty and staff to understand community needs better.

Garnering Alumni Support

Alumni organizations and alumni boards are populated by individuals who have a variety of motives for serving. As with other volunteer boards, members self-select based on their institutional loyalty and/or desire to enhance their résumé, a belief that they can improve their employment and business prospects, a need to participate in organized social functions, and/or any combination of these and other reasons. Individual board members' motives will shape the character and usefulness of the board and, by extension, the organization.

An alumni organization's participation in institutional life depends on its history and your ability to elicit its buy-in to your vision. Some organizations believe that their only functions are planning and executing alumni social events. Others participate in recruiting students and enhancing the reputation of the institution. Still others believe that they are a part of friend raising but not fund-raising. And, finally, some are full participants in the institutional development program.

Meet with the board and officers early in your tenure as president/chancellor. They may tell you exactly what they are and are not willing to do. If their expectations and yours differ significantly, accept their approach and expect to patiently bring them around to your point of view. This is not a group worth going to war with since they can be an integral part of your community support.

With respect to alumni, there are several tasks that will prove prudent for you:

1. Attend as many alumni events as possible. Make obvious your belief in their importance. It's also a proven way of getting to know an important segment of the community.
2. Carefully investigate the background and performance of the alumni director. Often, these organizations are responsible for large budgets and trust is important.
3. Support alumni involvement in university decisions. Often, they have good ideas, and their participation in a consultative environment can be very useful.
4. Invite select groups of alumni to university events. They will appreciate the attention and support you.
5. Continually praise the education afforded at the university, and use alumni as prominent examples to make your point.
6. When feasible, appoint alumni to search committees and task forces.
7. Alumni constitute an important constituency. Treat them that way, and they will repay your efforts many times over.

THE COMMUNITY AND THE WORLD

The institution's surrounding community and, indeed, the rest of the world are important from the related perspectives of resources and reputation. The local community can have a significant effect on day-to-day operations of an institution and affect tactical decisions. General reputation (the world's view of the institution) is a strategic issue and influences resources and enrollment.

Locally, several combinations of institutional size and community size are possible. And size matters. Four combinations are obvious: small campus/small community, large campus/small community, small campus/large community, large campus/large community.

In small communities, the institution (whether large or small) and the community can be extensively intertwined. Most often, there is only a single college or university in the town, and the town's well-being and that of the college or university are related. In such cases, it is in the best interest of the institution to maintain a positive relationship with the community, involving university employees in social organizations, not-for-profit organizations, schools, and even town governance. Further, it is important to ensure that student off-campus transgressions are not treated as unimportant and the college or university is seen as a good neighbor.

If the institution is large enough, the town's economic well-being is tied to the university's existence, which places the university in an unassailable bargaining position when controversies arise. In these cases, it is critical that the institution not act like the 500-pound gorilla, imposing its will on the community. Such behavior can sour town/gown relationships very quickly. Whether large or small, it is best if the institution acts like a partner, jointly solving problems, supporting community causes, and participating in community events.

When institutions, whether large or small, are part of large communities or cities, the dynamic changes. First, in most large cities, more than one college or university is present. This situation places the university in the position of vying for the community's favor and attention. Collaboration with community organizations and elected officials becomes even more important in ensuring the university's place in society. Offering consulting services, participating in joint projects, and inviting city officials to participate in advisory committees are all important in the collaboration effort. It is also appropriate to engage with other higher education institutions to collaborate with and support the community.

Further, in large communities, for the institution to become known and seen in a positive light, it is worthwhile to develop events and programs that bring the public into the university to become familiar with it and develop a kinship with the campus. It is important to convey to the nearby public that the campus is an asset, a positive influence, and has plenty to offer the community's citizens.

Where the rest of the world is concerned, it is necessary for the campus to develop its reputation, especially to attract students and other support. Of course, rating organizations such as *US News & World Report* have their place in defining reputation, but most important are those who come into contact with you and your campus.

First, students having good experiences and talking about them are your best advertisements. Second, employees being satisfied with the usefulness and importance of their work and the institution's caring about them is conveyed wherever they travel. Third, anyone having contact with the campus should have a good experience whether the individuals are prospective students or employees, suppliers, contractors, visitors, or elected officials. Fourth, international visitors and students convey the campus image to the world, and their having positive experiences is worth ensuring. And finally, it helps if the campus public relations organization conveys the same message as well.

Campus image, both local and extended, garners friends and supporters, which in turn helps bring resources to the campus.

Suggestions for Ensuring Positive Campus and Community Relations

The communities in which universities find themselves vary widely in size, opportunity, and attitude toward the institution. However, no matter what opinion the community has of the university, it can exert strong and immediate positive or negative influences on the institution. In this environment, universities ignore communities' character, needs, and attitudes at their peril.

Students, faculty, and staff live in the community. Their individual behaviors will shape community attitudes toward the institution. Several suggestions might be helpful:

1. When incidents occur, do not respond immediately. Make sure that you know the relevant facts before forming an opinion.
2. If students cause physical damage in the community, negotiate appropriate restitution and allow either the community or the university judicial system to do their work.
3. Broker mutual support agreements and attitudes between university and local law enforcement. Do not allow a situation to evolve where, when local law enforcement is pursuing a student, university law enforcement gives sanctuary to the pursued.
4. Use mutual support agreements as the basis for further cooperation. Local law enforcement can be very helpful if pockets of drug culture spring up in proximity to the campus. When serious illegalities occur (homicide, rape, robbery, mugging), local law enforcement will supply resources and trained personnel that university police most often do not have. And campus police can provide support personnel, when needed, to local police.
5. Never brush off any situation with a "kids will be kids" defense. Someone has taken the incident seriously and will be offended.
6. To the extent possible, do not become involved when faculty or staff members transgress in the community unless there is a glar-

ing injustice. If the behavior reflects badly on the institution, rely on reminding the community of institutional values and your support of behavior that models those values.

The community often needs help and support. Follow a basic principle: When the community asks for help, try to help. Several examples might be instructive:

1. United Way and other social service campaigns are often community cornerstones. Get involved! If you don't, community members will use your behavior as a reason to deny private donations to the institution.
2. Welcome the community to university events. Athletic and arts events are the most obvious examples. However, lectures, celebrations, and convocations are attractive to some in the community.
3. If not enjoined by regulation, offer the library as a community asset.
4. Host community events on campus.

Your goal should be to encourage the community to feel that the institution is as much a part of them as their parks and other community assets are.

Another important realization is that the community's rules and regulations often apply to campus projects. So zoning laws, building inspection rules, utilities easements, and a host of other issues can be problematic if the institution's relationship with the community is rocky. Negotiating a community's bureaucracy can be significantly simplified if the relationship with city and county officials is strong. So it is important to build personal bonds with those individuals.

Recognize them at campus events. Allow them to speak and be visible where appropriate. Cultivate them as you would donors. Your attention to them will pay off.

Bringing Constituencies Together

Universities occupy a unique place in their communities. Simultaneously, they are a significant part of the educational infrastructure, major contributors to the economy, a repository of expertise and knowledge that could be applied to community problems, a cultural force, and a community within the community, among other roles.

That set of critical roles allows the president/chancellor to play a leading role in bringing constituencies together both to achieve mutual understandings and to seek solutions to community problems. Recognizing where and when to exercise this power is an important talent that a campus leader must develop.

Several examples make the point. Imagine the contribution a university can make when a community is deeply involved in economic development. The business, sociological, technical, and other skills available at the university as well as the volunteer time of executives can be invaluable in making economic development programs successful.

Now, imagine the university expertise that could be applied to problems involving community youth, water quality, energy conservation, information technology services, and a host of other issues. Involvement in United Way campaigns and other community social service projects is another example of constituencies working together.

It is the president's/chancellor's unique position and ability to focus the resources of the institution as well as to orchestrate collaboration among community organizations that can build community loyalty to the institution. And it is that loyalty that results in financial support, positive town/gown relationships, and positive responses when tensions inevitably rise between the university and its host community.

EIGHT

Institutional Structures, Organizations, and Responsibilities

ATHLETICS

The promise, pitfalls, politics, and pedantry of athletics can absorb almost all of a president's/chancellor's time and energy if he or she so chooses. The promise of athletics includes greater visibility for the institution, more student and alumni loyalty, increased community support and enrollment, and enhanced donations. The pitfalls include income shortfalls, faculty enmity, and rules and ethics violations, which can negate all of the promise. The politics include conference interactions, board oversight, donor and fan relations, and NCAA relationships. The pedantry includes athletics' slavish attention to statistics and tradition, the faculty's nearly religious focus on criticizing athletics, and your need to continually monitor the program's commitment to its own enhancement.

    Let's begin with the promise of athletics. In American society, athletics has dominated media as well as casual conversation for decades. As a result, it appears that developing a successful athletics program is a path to institutional fame (or infamy) and fortune (or loss) as well as student and alumni loyalty. Just speak to athletics directors of programs sporting winning records or long traditions, and you will find quick agreement with the premise. In fact, single winning seasons in basketball, football, or even volleyball, if well publicized, can result in stronger general enrollments at and general interest in the institution.

    Further, boosters will open their wallets or pocketbooks, as the case may be, if they feel positively about the program. And that financial support can often spill over into support for other aspects of a college campus, whether academic, social, or otherwise. In addition, the campus environment can be significantly enhanced by having successful teams, which engender campus spirit and generally positive feelings about the campus. So supporting a successful athletics program can have its rewards.

But the pits into which you and the institution can fall are deep and dangerous. First, if the program is not successful (if your teams don't win), not only do your boosters and fans become tepid in their support, but media can initiate a groundswell of criticism that is both embarrassing and destructive.

For reasons buried deep in American culture and psychology, we all expect and want to support winners, in spite of the fact that in almost every contest, there is a winner and a loser. As a result, when our teams don't win, we are disappointed, become morose, and oftentimes withhold support and demand that heads roll until a winning combination is found. The consequence for the unsuccessful program is diminished financial support and enhanced negative publicity, leading to further diminished financial support and enhanced negative publicity. The downward trend can be both quick and steep. And it is also important to remember that nationally, few athletics programs show a positive cash flow. Only if all of the variables are included—cash flow, enrollment, image, general support, and tradition—can an institution justify supporting such a program.

At the same time, it is important to remember that the tradition related to institutions having athletics programs can be outweighed by the traditions surrounding faculty criticizing athletics programs. Not only do faculty members expect that the programs be free from scandal, they also expect that athletes will perform at least as well as the general student body academically. And if the athletics program invests significantly in academic support, faculty expects athletes to outperform the general student body. Falling short of reasonable academic performance can also lead to major problems in athletics.

Further, financially troubled programs that require university subsidy can engender intense faculty enmity resulting from the members' belief that the subsidy could have supported them. As university financial woes expand, who can blame them?

And finally, expectations for success often lead to ethical lapses and rules violations that can devastate a program. To be sure, the NCAA regulations are so thick with rules that inadvertently contravening one or another can occur at any time. Unfortunately, in search of the perfect athlete, to gain specific advantage, or to ensure that athletes are trained to their maximum potential, coaches, boosters, and athletics program officials, or even unrelated university officials, will willfully breach the rules to help the program succeed. No president/chancellor can fully ensure that such violations will not occur, but he or she can manage the risk to a certain extent.

First, do not hire people into the athletics program who have any history of unprofessional or unethical conduct or a history of NCAA rules violations. Second, in programs that employ a compliance officer, insist that that position report directly to you. That structure relieves the athletics director of the conflict between winning and following the rules, since the position charged with enforcement and rules compliance no longer reports within the program. Of course, you cannot completely protect yourself or your institution from problems, but you can manage the risk. By the way, none of these suggestions have any hope of helping if you, yourself, do not behave ethically.

The politics of athletics is arcane, complex, and petty, much like politics anywhere. Within the athletics department, coaches vie for position and favor, both personally and for their sport. Winning is an indisputable bottom line for them, because their continued employment often depends directly on their win/loss record. So their willingness to cross ethical lines and ability to manipulate are often enhanced.

Athletics directors also base their continuation on winning and losing, but also rise and fall on their ability to maintain financial viability and avoid problems. They must deal with faculty, administrative, and donor factions; conference conflicts and demands; and the NCAA or NAIA. So their entire existence is politically motivated.

Presidents/chancellors must deal with all of the campus factions, as well as the NCAA or NAIA, donors, and the presidents/chancellors of universities both within the athletics conference and in the NCAA or NAIA. Unfortunately, within athletics conferences, the worst of presidential behaviors is manifested, as ethical behavior takes a holiday in favor of political expediency, during discussions of income distribution, new members, championship revenues, and eligibility rules.

Finally, the pedantry of athletics takes its toll. The NCAA's slavish attention to rules enforcement and the letter of the rules forces institutions and their leaders to act similarly. And just as the NCAA employs a massive rules enforcement staff, institutions are similarly obligated to both hire and train staff to maintain compliance. And this in turn engenders a reporting system that requires the time and attention of all involved.

Further, the slavish attention of athletics itself to statistics, win/loss records, and other details requires time and attention as well.

While these four athletics "P's" (promise, pitfalls, politics, and pedantry) require presidential focus, most CEOs believe that the promise of athletics far outweighs the pitfalls, since athletics has been such a traditional part of higher education. However, problems in the athletics program can as quickly shorten the tenure of a president/chancellor as any other aspect of institutional life. One athletics director suggested three principles on which to base a successful athletics program: academic integrity, social responsibility, and athletics intensity, prioritized in that order. He probably stole the concept from someone else, but it clearly indicates an ethically unassailable path, and the approach makes sense.

Athletics People: The Sharks Swim Quietly and Deeply

Realizing that people, both internally and externally, involved in athletics programs are motivated by nearly irresistible forces may help clarify your dealing with the programs and their problems. And accepting that the welfare of student athletes both individually and as teams is the bottom line may help focus your efforts.

The success of any team or program depends on the talents and attitudes of individual athletes. The typical student athlete enters college at age eighteen or nineteen, is subject to all the hormonal imperatives of that age cohort, has been pressured by parents and/or society throughout a significant portion of his or her life to use athletics participation as a path to lifelong success or to acquire an affordable education, and is new to the freedom that attending college affords.

Ordinarily, they will exit their college athletics career educated and having learned important lessons about teamwork, time management, loyalty, and themselves. And during that intervening four years they will have experienced the emotional highs and lows typical of that age of human beings. It is those mood swings that can determine whether a game or match is won or lost; a team enjoys or lacks cohesion; and in the grand scheme of things, a coach, an athletics director, or an athletics program is successful.

Coaches' careers depend on whether their teams win or lose. So to ensure success, they recruit the best athletes possible. The competition for those athletes is fierce, and a coach feels incredible pressure to use every means possible to succeed, including ignoring rules and their violations by assistant coaches. And after successfully recruiting those student athletes, the coach must not only meld them into a successful team but must also ensure that their academic performance is such that they remain eligible, don't get involved with drugs and alcohol, and appropriately represent the institution.

It is not surprising that many coaches are self-centered, selfish on behalf of their teams, and often socially awkward. It is also not surprising that due to the instability of their positions and the importance of their teams to the institutions, they demand extraordinary compensation.

Athletics directors experience similar pressures but on a grander scale. They must deal with the coaches, rules, student athletes, and public while balancing the financial issues attendant to athletics. They must also deal with athletics conferences, athletics directors from competing institutions, and the media to be successful. As a result, they feel forced to hire large staffs to deal with the complexity of the operation, further increasing the financial pressure on the athletics organization.

Finally, they must also manage relations with donors and fans who are generous and supportive when teams are winning but unforgiving and critical when teams are less successful. It should come as no surprise that many athletics directors fall victim to whatever brand of situational ethics gives them comfort and they suffer the resulting reputations.

Overlaying all of this with donor and fan relations, faculty distrust of and disgust with athletics, media reporting on athletics in preference to the rest of the institution, legislative and board meddling, and any of a number of other factors yield the environment and set of circumstances that are the president's/chancellor's responsibilities. The problems and issues can expand to fill your entire day.

Keeping athletics in perspective is a daunting task. It helps to remember that the complexities, issues, and responsibilities all depend on the hormonal swings of eighteen- to twenty-two-year-old student athletes and their well-being is your responsibility.

PLANNING: STRATEGIC AND OTHERWISE

Planning, strategic or otherwise, is the sine qua non of any executive position. If there are no goals, there is no vision, no definition of progress, and little incentive to excel, and the organization languishes. If you're the president/chancellor of an institution, you already know this. If you do not, your common sense has dissipated, or you had none when you assumed the position. And though planning in an organization is critical, there is no single way of going about it.

However, there are several aspects of planning that are worth considering.

At its simplest, planning consists of three steps: determining goals or outcomes, evaluating alternative ways of reaching those goals, and choosing courses of action. In vogue these days is strategic planning. But there are multiple kinds of planning: strategic, tactical, operational, short term, long term, and contingency, among many others. Each has utility, but the businesspeople who control most higher education boards of trustees have become enamored of strategic planning.

All planning comprises the three steps mentioned before. Strategic planning, while involving all stakeholders in an organization, formally determines an institutional mission, creates a vision for the institution, defines the values within which the institution will operate in pursuit of the vision and mission, and describes the strategies it will use to achieve its vision including goals and objectives to be met on the way to those goals. Then once a strategic plan is crafted, its success is measured according to a set of metrics defined within the plan. Constructs such as dashboards and balanced scorecards are often used to collect and analyze the metrics.

But it's relatively easy to put the elements of a strategic plan in place. While choosing words to describe visions, goals, and values can eat up time and energy, the final result, the success of the plan, and therefore the organization, will be determined by the quality and intensity of involvement of all stakeholders, the extent to which the vision is shared, and the monitoring of, attention to, and adjustment of the plan during its execution. Too many strategic plans, once written, sit on a shelf throughout the planning period, only to be removed from the shelf and evaluated after the planning horizon, usually five years.

Since most academic institutions have, in the main, the same mission—teaching, research, and service—and most make some progress during a five-year period, unless their enrollment falls off a cliff, paying little attention to the plan and evaluating progress at the end often occurs. However, institutions make progress by setting reasonable goals, monitoring progress continually, and adjusting the plan and approaches along the way.

Fundamentally, a campus leader is planning continually. It's tactical planning with respect to individual issues. It's contingency planning for crisis. It's succession planning for leadership at all levels. It's organizational planning to adjust the institutional structure. In fact, asleep, awake, in the shower, exercising, during the day and at night, a leader is always planning.

Leaders (presidents/chancellors) and, therefore, organizations succeed when the organization's constituencies believe they are part of and therefore buy in to the goals, values, and tactics set forth during a planning process. For this to happen, the results of the planning processes must be communicated to all constituencies.

Managing a Strategic Planning Process

Strategic planning is an exercise in which the execution of the process is as important as the final product. If participants do not feel invested in and are not contributors to the published plan, no matter how brilliant and promising that plan is, the execution of the plan will fail. And as a corollary, no matter how inclusive the planning process is, if the plan is shelved and not monitored, the goals will remain unrealized. Thus, several suggestions result:

1. Lead the process leading to the completed plan. Do not delegate leadership.
2. Involve representatives of as many institutional constituencies as possible in the planning process.
3. Communicate often and extensively during the process with the constituencies either through the representatives or directly.

4. Organize enough meetings so there is enough personal interaction that participants become well acquainted but few enough meetings so the process is not a burdensome imposition.
5. Charter a group that will monitor the final plan during its term. One clever acronym for such a group is SPARC (Strategic Planning Assessment and Review Committee).
6. Insist that the monitoring committee meet regularly to discuss plan progress and suggest improvements.

The plan itself is an important leadership and management tool. Since the process yields a document crafted by a broad spectrum of interested parties, it becomes not only a blueprint for future progress but also a framework with which to justify new initiatives. As long as a proposed change can be linked to the spirit and general goals of the plan, it bears the imprimatur of the plan and is more easily defended against those who believe any change is bad.

EQUITY AND COMPLIANCE

Of the many values that any higher education institution might list in its portfolio, equity—fair and impartial treatment of all involved—should be among those held most important. If higher education stands for anything, it should stand for equal opportunity and equal treatment so that each member of the community can achieve in accordance with his or her ability and commitment, neither of which will ever be equal among individuals.

So the first responsibility of a leader of such an institution is to model expected institutional behavior. Where equity is concerned, your behavior will be the first example employees and students consider in determining their own. But simply modeling the behavior is not enough. It's your responsibility to ensure that the expected behavior permeates the entire organization. Accomplishing that requires a set of policies and procedures that follow state and federal laws, an equity/equal opportunity compliance office, and a campus-wide attitude (based on the president's/chancellor's behavior) that work together in an integrated fashion.

Choosing a chief equity officer isn't a trivial undertaking, because while many applicants may have the necessary credentials, few have the appropriate attitude. With respect to qualifications, applicants who have legal training seem to fare best; however, experienced human resource professionals can provide excellent service. No matter what training applicants have, they must be attentive to detail; empathetic but not biased; logical, especially in situations where investigations are necessary; thorough, and above all, possess a deeply held belief that employees and students should advance according to their ability without being subject to bias, harassment, hostility, or any other form of unfair treatment.

It is also important that an equity officer be patient and not rush to judgment before an investigation has been completed, although in some egregious situations, an employee must be placed on leave to prevent further damage. Finally, the equity officer must be able to step back from the situation to maintain neutrality, and lawyers seem to be more able to accomplish this than practitioners from other professions.

Overseeing the development of policies and procedures related to equity is another responsibility of the president/chancellor. Whether ensuring that current policies and procedures are functional and effective or developing new documents, having legal advice is mandatory to be in compliance with applicable policies, regulations, and laws. In that instance, having a chief equity officer who has legal training is beneficial.

Further, it is often the responsibility of the president/chancellor to be the final or near final adjudicator of complaints. Adhering carefully to procedures makes provision of due process a reality for complainant and respondent. Once again, employing an equity officer who has legal training and whose advice you are willing to take is an advantage since procedures can be complex and easily breached.

To ensure equity or equal opportunity, hiring procedures throughout the institution must be consistent and fair. Having the chief equity officer take responsibility for fairness in the hiring process can make this a reality; however, many institutions assign equity-in-hiring responsibilities to human resources or, in the case of faculty, to academic affairs.

The equity officer is also responsible for a great deal of counseling, listening, and emotional support for students and staff. And while that might not seem like a great responsibility, it may be the most important one in minimizing formal complaints and maximizing employee satisfaction and security.

Finally, and once again, it is your behavior that serves as the model for all others, including the equity officer. And modeling appropriate behavior, especially where equity is concerned, has profound influence on the entire institution.

Ensuring Equity on Campus

"Campus equity" has two related but distinct meanings. Formally, it refers to the set of administrative processes set in place to allow aggrieved parties to seek redress, especially where discrimination with regard to ethnicity, race, gender, LGBTQ, and related issues has occurred. However, informally, it refers to the set of campus attitudes and behaviors that combine to create an environment in which individuals believe they are being fairly treated in all aspects of campus life.

Formal equity is ensured at an institution when you charter the set of policies and processes required by law and tradition and then supervise their execution. Oversite is usually accomplished using a combination of the campus equity office, human resources, a legal team, a student judicial system, and appropriate administrators. The processes and policies employed depend on the institution and individuals involved. Achieving formal equity is not difficult, because succeeding in creating the formal system requires only your time and attention and the will to do it.

Informal equity is much more difficult to achieve. And it is developed from the top down. It is your behavior as president/chancellor that creates an environment where faculty, staff, and students believe that whatever challenge confronts them, they can expect fair treatment. The content of your speeches, treatment of people, offhand comments, and presence on campus, among other things, meld to form the model for the rest of the campus.

Treating faculty, staff, and students with respect and sensitivity empowers your administration and the rest of the campus to behave similarly. But be careful! Your uttering an insensitive, offhand remark; attempting humor that is inadvertently offensive; or brushing off an individual can result in a news item that will infect the campus. Each of these events negates the positive effect of numerous kind and appropriate words and actions.

The best outcome and highest praise you can expect in this arena is for faculty, staff, and students to say, "We always knew he or she had our backs!"

Encouraging Diversity

If the equity office is the lynchpin concept leading to campus perceptions of fairness, then diversity is one measure of effectiveness of the equity office. And diversity ought to be what a university education is about. So your role in promoting diversity is more important than any other. It is your passionate belief in diversity's power that helps lead others to a similar set of values.

In that regard, visibility, commitment, and support are important behaviors. Being a visible presence at diversity-promoting events, attending meetings of campus organizations promoting diversity, and being a part of celebrations such as Kwanza, Chinese New Year and Moon Festival, Cinco de Mayo, and others contribute to visibility. And visibility is part of being seen as committed to diversity, but it's not the entire picture of commitment.

Commitment also includes being vocal concerning hiring a diverse workforce and attracting a diverse student body and then acting on those statements, especially in the composition of your direct reports and those for whom you are a part of the hiring process. Just as visibility is part of commitment, commitment is part of support. However, support includes obvious organizational financial support and the time commitment of employees. It is critical that if and when budget issues become prominent, diversity efforts are not the first to be cut.

It is also critical that campus diversity extends to diversity of thought, expression, opinion, and belief. Celebration of diversity of faith is a given on most campuses. However, sensitivity to other religious beliefs is often forgotten or overlooked when, for example, prayers are offered in Jesus's name. Such faux pas are easily remedied. However, not so easily fixed are the intolerances relating to diversity of thought and expression.

Consider the liberal professor who is intolerant of conservative viewpoints, the student whose commitment to right to life is so intense that she cannot tolerate other viewpoints during class discussion, the atheist professor who denigrates any organized religion's beliefs and practices, or the right- or left-leaning student group that interrupts a campus speaker espousing a point of view contrary to its own. These are behaviors that have no place on campus, where the purpose of the organization is open discussion in search of intellectual enlightenment.

As the chief executive, it is the president's/chancellor's obligation to ensure that diversity not only of race, gender, religion, and lifestyle is celebrated but also that the celebration extends to diversity of thought and expression.

MANAGING ENROLLMENT

For most academic institutions, enrollment levels determine a large fraction of the income available to the organization. For small institutions, small student enrollment swings can determine whether the annual budget is made or not. For large institutions, enrollment swings can be in the hundreds of students without affecting the budget. However, whether an institution is large or small, accurately predicting and monitoring enrollment is an important leadership responsibility because institutional income affects the well-being of students, faculty, and staff as well as that of the institution.

So enrollment management, the structure and process for controlling enrollment levels, is important if not critical to an institution. Just how critical managing enrollment is determines whether the function should report to the president/chancellor or to some lower level within the institution. Having it report to the CEO sends a message about its importance to the institution and helps those responsible for its success feel more invested. Having it report elsewhere sends a different message.

Organizationally, what is enrollment management? Fundamentally, enrollment depends on two functions, attracting students to the institution and retaining them once they're there. Many factors determine an institution's ability to attract and retain students, so several areas of the institution are involved in the effort. In many institutions, these areas are separated or in silos, resulting in the need for integrated enrollment management—managing enrollment by coordinating and making mutually supportive multiple institutional operations.

Attracting students to the institution requires coordination of several campus functions. Mainly, the impression given potential students results from the work of admissions and university relations. However, that impression is formed based on the institution's image, academic, physical, and otherwise. Responsible organizations include admissions, registrar, student life, athletics, university relations, and to a lesser extent, even physical plant and custodial services. Therefore, the core of an enrollment management organization might include admissions, registrar, and the organization responsible for new student orientation. Collaboration would then be required of other organizations. The structure needs to comport with institutional culture.

Where retention is concerned, academic areas, student life, and counseling and advising services are all involved. Thus an enrollment management organization might also include counseling and advising and even some part of student life, but the academic functions are best left in academic affairs.

However, there is a less organizational, more environmental aspect of retention that merits discussion. A student's remaining at an institution often depends on whether he or she feels cared for or cared about. And that feeling depends on an attitude prevalent at the institution. When a student has problems, is he or she ignored or bounced from one office to another? Are clerical and reception staff members helpful, or are they dismissive or hostile to students? Is the campus welcoming, or does a student feel like part of the landscape?

How students "feel" about the campus is absolutely critical, and the enrollment management organization must have sufficient leadership capability, enough gravitas, and be prominent enough to create a positive environment that both attracts and retains students.

Enrollment is important, and it must be attended to and managed in such a way as to support the success of the institution. Several suggestions for organizing enrollment management might be helpful:

1. Choose a leader for the enrollment management organization who enjoys the respect necessary for genuine collaboration to occur.
2. Consider the possibility of your leading the effort with the help of strong deputies.
3. Insist on development of a plan appropriate to the culture of the institution and ensure that attention is paid to following and constantly improving it.
4. Make sure that a senior member of the organization possesses the mathematical and communication skills to understand, interpret, and report data.

5. Recognize and reward successful innovations.

MAINTAINING THE PHYSICAL PLANT

When students visit a college or university for the first time, no matter how much they have known previously about the campus, the impression that the campus itself makes is very important. Consciously or unconsciously students' first impressions can be "This looks like I dreamed a campus would!" or "They don't maintain this place very well!" or "I'm going to spend four years here?" The appearance of a campus can, therefore, have a direct effect on enrollment.

Similarly, the appearance of the campus, how well it's maintained, and how clean it is has a direct effect on faculty and staff morale. Trash removal, litter pickup, and restroom cleaning, if not attended to, can drive employee attitudes about the campus and influence job performance.

So keeping the people responsible for the physical aspects of a campus committed and satisfied needs to be a priority for the president/chancellor. Every employee of the institution should be helped to feel that his or her job is important and, as long as they do the job, the president/chancellor will keep it secure. This is especially true for service personnel. The campus needs for them to develop both pride in doing their jobs well and loyalty to the campus.

It is critical that service personnel maintain this pride, because students and other staff interact with them and their positive attitudes are also integral to the mosaic that comprises the general campus environment. Thus campus personnel responsible for the physical aspects of the campus are dually responsible for the appearance of the campus and contributing to overall campus attitude.

Many presidents/chancellors believe that their interaction with service personnel is unimportant or goes unnoticed. However, every instance in which the campus CEO speaks personally to a custodian, police officer, or maintenance or ground person is noted and discussed. And the authenticity of those interactions is judged. Further, the campus leader should seek opportunities to praise and/or support service personnel since they seldom receive much recognition for their efforts. Award ceremonies, staff luncheons, and second- and third-shift events are all opportunities to help staff feel valued and important.

In general, it is important to remember that all staff members are your responsibility, not just those with whom you feel most comfortable.

Maintaining the Physical Environment

Service personnel interact with students, staff, and faculty often, and the results of their work can directly affect campus culture and attitudes. Service staff attitudes can be directly affected by how the president/chancellor treats them. Several suggestions might help:

1. At staff awards ceremonies, personally present the awards and shake awardees' hands. While you may not know much about many of them, a few words of recognition about the ones you do will go a long way toward garnering support for and loyalty to the campus.
2. When you walk around campus, take time to greet service workers. When possible, greet them by name. Compliment their work if appropriate.
3. Mention the quality of service personnel's work and commitment in speeches.
4. Don't forget to recognize the contributions of second- and third-shift personnel.
5. Make sure that service staff members are provided with the tools to do their jobs. When budget cuts occur, this is often the area affected. The investment is small and the payoff is large.

PUBLIC RELATIONS

Everybody's advertising these days. Doctors, lawyers, drug companies, and educational institutions are all out hawking their wares. Two generations ago, such behavior was deemed unseemly and unprofessional. Professionals simply did not lower themselves to compete at those levels. However, it has become common for a college to advertise that it is more flexible, transparent, fun, academic, and so on than any other college; community colleges to advertise that they are cheaper and will direct students to better jobs; and state universities to claim that they are more comprehensive and offer better value than their private counterparts do. In general, public relations and advertising budgets in higher education have soared, as has the effort expended in worrying about the competition.

These efforts are most often housed in an area called university relations or communications or public relations, among others, and staffed by public relations professionals. Institutions have come to the belief that their reputation and attractiveness are directly dependent on the work of their public relations professionals. And that the more resources invested in branding, marketing, and public relations efforts, the better off an institution will be. Thus, stories of successes are hyperbolized, and stories of failures are minimized. And the overall reputation of the institution and its effectiveness are lost in the noise.

Similarly, institutions manipulate inputs to rating organizations such as *US News & World Report* to enhance their standings. As a result, not unlike the results of SATs, the ratings are accurate for the top 5 percent of institutions and virtually meaningless for the rest.

And they buy billboards and radio and TV time to ensure their visibility. Further enhancing that visibility is participation in NCAA Division I athletics and competing in postseason play.

All in, this investment in time and money may escalate into millions of dollars and multiple professional staff years. In the current environment, it would be foolish for a university to consider jettisoning its PR operation. Thus, the investment must be maintained. However, greater honesty and transparency might be in order.

A university's reputation ought to be based on the success and satisfaction of its graduates, reputation of its faculty, and results of its support to its surrounding community. In an open and authentic way, the institution can share such information, but most have difficulty sharing it without spin or exaggeration. It would almost be refreshing if institutions made available accurate, rather than biased, information.

On a related note, media relations are often problematic for institutions. It is incredibly easy to become defensive with either print or mass media, especially when reporters are probing for answers in rude or confronting ways. An effective means of dealing with media is to maintain continual contact, whether there's news or crisis or not, thus ensuring that when news of crisis is prominent, the reporters and institutional representatives know each other well. Similarly, with editorial boards, meeting with them regularly helps ensure both the accuracy of their opinions and receiving fair treatment when crises occur.

When crises do occur, getting out in front of the story is an effective means of keeping the issues from getting out of hand. And informing reporters before they engage in chasing a story helps the institution get fair treatment. Further, when reporters ask questions, remembering that they have deadlines and responding in a timely fashion is usually very much appreciated.

A corollary approach is useful where external constituencies are concerned. Keeping the community informed about the campus, its structure, challenges, and general condition, will go a long way toward obtaining sympathetic treatment when a real issue comes up.

Ensuring That University Relations Creates More Feast than Famine

University relations touches all areas of the institution and usually expends most of its efforts publicizing successes. But successful programs and efforts in one area can invite the enmity of another. The classic example of this phenomenon is publicity surrounding athletics achievements or lack of same. It is easier to get media attention for athletics than it is for any other university effort, unless your medical school discovers a cure for cancer or one of your faculty creates a viable plan to achieve world peace. Thus, faculty and sometimes other staff will take issue with the publicity afforded athletics.

Enmities can also develop among faculty members if one department receives more attention than another or among staff if student programming is more prominent than academic achievement. Common in this regard are faculty members in the humanities and sciences taking issue with the media attention afforded the arts. So it is important to try to reach a balance in publicizing university programs and for university relations to be perceived as evenhanded in its efforts.

University relations can also be responsible for responding to media inquiries, whether related to positive or negative incidents on the campus. Responses to any questions about campus events should be consistent with institutional policies and priorities, and personnel who interact with the media should be adequately trained. If questions arise concerning emergent situations, senior officials should be knowledgeable, and agreements should have been reached about who would speak for the institution. Whether spokespeople are from university relations or are other university officials, the decision must be made and enforced to ensure a consistent message.

Decisions about the role of university relations in emergent situations should result from a carefully managed university emergency planning process. That process could be executed by university relations but should be led by you. Whatever the outcome of a campus emergency, responsibility will be laid directly at your doorstep. Your direct involvement in emergency planning will help you to weather any storm that results.

Finally, and most important, is the responsibility of university relations to the institution as a whole. It is fairly common for the staff of university relations to become so absorbed in the day-to-day tactics surrounding promoting the institution that they minimize efforts to develop the institutional brand and the overall image of the university or college. The institutional brand is the starting point for attracting students, faculty, and staff to the university, and it is an important part of the foundation on which institutional self-image is built.

An institution's brand comprises the first thought an individual has when the name of the college or university is mentioned and the image the institution's name invokes. It is the emotional response to discussion of its merits based on the individual's life experience and experience with the institution. It is related to reputation, but that's not the whole story because reputation is a group opinion, the positive nature of which is the result of brand management.

Many universities advertise. Many undertake sophisticated and expensive public relations campaigns. Few understand that it is the institution's brand that requires careful examination and management. If you are considering a significant investment in an advertising and public relations campaign, hire reputable, professional help to guide your efforts and remember that brand management should be the goal of your effort.

One more suggestion might be useful. Avoid changing long-standing names, logos, colors, representations, or mascots, unless you have organized universal buy-in. Many institutional ships and individual careers have foundered on the shoals of a changed mascot or other emotionally charged symbol. Don't let yours be one of them.

Speeches and Remarks: Public Appearances

Often, the public relations organization is responsible for writing remarks for the president/chancellor. Don't fall into this trap unless it is crystal clear that you do not have the time or the knowledge to write them. There are two important reasons for following this advice:

1. Unless your PR organization has writers who are so talented or have been with you so long that they can write in your voice, the speeches will not sound like you and your delivery will be stilted. Further, your audience will wonder who wrote the remarks rather than listening to the message.
2. Often, speech writers are writing against deadlines, and no matter how hard they and you try to avoid the situation, the speech will be handed to you five minutes before the presentation. Unless you are one of the most talented improvisers and/or sight readers in the Western world, the event becomes an accident waiting to happen. You will inevitably stumble over unrehearsed words and phrases, and the audience will almost certainly miss your major points.

Several approaches help avoid this chain of events:

1. Practice delivering and then deliver some presentations extemporaneously. Make sure you have the facts right. Use your PR organization to prepare you. This approach will allow you to develop a reputation for extemporaneous erudition as well as allowing an audience to hear your opinions in your voice.
2. When more formal presentations are in order, task your PR organization with preparing organized talking points and then tie them together with your own words.
3. For really formal occasions, don't be afraid to read a speech. When reading, ensure that you know the material, deliver it smoothly,

and using your own words, deliver the speech in a believable manner.
4. Avoid delivering speeches that consist of quotations from well-known people strung together with platitudes. The audience wants to hear what you think, not what some long-dead celebrity thought. If you insist on using quotes, find obscure quotes attributed to individuals who enjoy impeccable respect. Remember that few in the audience for your speeches will be interested in what Tom Cruise, Taylor Swift, or Sean Connery have to say.

ACCREDITATION

Regional accrediting agencies act to ensure that entire colleges and universities are educating their students in a way that makes consistent the definitions of associate's, bachelor's, master's, and doctoral degrees. In that way, those who hire graduates of higher educational institutions can expect some normalization in the meaning of the degree a graduate has earned and the skills he or she has learned.

The mechanism common to accreditation consists of the agency appointing a team of peer reviewers who visit the college or university (usually once every ten years if all is in order). That team creates a report concerning whether the university is meeting a set of predetermined standards. If the standards are met, the team recommends a ten-year revisit along with other helpful suggestions. Other outcomes, depending on the severity of the shortfall, could be one-, three-, or five-year revisits or submission of a report detailing solutions to problems, or some combination of the two.

Whichever regional accreditation agency is involved, it is important to remember that accreditation is serious business and must be near top of mind at all times. Preparing for accreditation should be continual, although it is difficult not to take a two- or three-year break after a ten-year visit. Paying attention to assessment and strategic planning will help to cause the necessary attention to accreditation and the necessary preparation to occur.

When a ten-year accreditation visit is imminent, it is worthwhile to consider several issues. Look carefully at team credentials. Challenge the service of those members who serve at institutions that are so unlike yours that they will not understand the function at your institution. Having a Yale accreditor evaluating Downstate Technical College is problematic, as is the reverse.

There will inevitably be one team member who criticizes everything during the visit. Sometimes this is simply a personality quirk, and the team member will provide competent input. Sometimes team members believe it is their role to be difficult. Sometimes the member is genuinely not pleased about what he or she sees. Whatever the case, treat all team members similarly, courteously and professionally, and work any problems out when you have an opportunity to respond to their report. Finally, treat team members as honored guests on campus. The courtesy will pay off.

Discipline-specific accreditation teams are a slightly different animal. These individuals consider themselves experts in their fields and sometimes behave arrogantly in that regard. Often, such members are interpersonally difficult and can cause a visit to be a nightmare. The best advice in this situation is to trust your own faculty experts and treat the team members professionally, no matter how difficult they are. Some of the agencies they represent are extremely powerful and can cause a great deal of trouble for your programs. The National League for Nursing (NLN), Accreditation Board for Engineering and Technology (ABET), and Association to Advance Collegiate Schools of Business (AACSB) are examples. Some have little authority, and loss of their accreditation is less meaningful. The American Chemical Society (ACS) is an example. Whichever one applies, learn about each agency and treat its reviewers accordingly.

Organizing an Accreditation Experience: The Report and the Visit

Preparing for an accreditation visit requires attention to detail on two fronts, report preparation and visit organization. Ordinarily, report preparation consists of a yearlong effort that is executed by a broadly based committee led by a faculty member or academic administrator. Important also is the extensive involvement of staff from Institutional Research. Whether the accreditation is institutional or discipline based, the accrediting agency provides a set of report guidelines, adhering to which is not rocket science. However, the report should continually refer back to the institutional strategic plan.

The second preparation responsibility is the organization of the visit. This task should not be trusted to report preparation committee members because the attention to detail and courtesies necessary are usually not in their skill set. It is important to ensure that none of the physical details of the visit are left to chance. Accreditation team members tend to respond poorly to glitches in local transportation, meeting rooms that are not properly outfitted, schedules that are not met, shabby accommodations, or any of a number of other issues that have nothing to do with institutional quality but can have subtle and overt effects on the final report.

Finally, remember that yours is probably not among the twenty most prominent universities in the United States. Accreditation team members might allow shortcomings to slip by at those institutions, but they will not at yours. Care in report preparation and involvement of the entire campus in the process is your best path to identifying shortfalls and fixing them.

INSTITUTIONAL RESEARCH

Institutional research (IR) can be an important asset to a president/chancellor or it can be completely useless. In extreme cases, it can be a significant negative issue for the CEO. Institutional research, the organization that produces and, in many cases, analyzes institutional data, should reach broadly across university organizations, providing data on all aspects of university life. If it is to provide interpretation and analysis as well as advice on data collection, it must be staffed with professionals well versed in the institutional research profession. Unfortunately, many IR divisions become repositories for administrators who have not been stellar performers in other areas. While these personnel might be expert in institutional history and organization, their skills in statistical analysis and operations research are not well developed. So the needed data and interpretations might not be forthcoming from an organization so constituted.

On the other hand, an organization populated by IR professionals and led well can be an immense asset. In both internal and external communication the CEO's most effective tools comprise information about the institution. And quantitative information makes arguments much more powerful.

As an organization, IR can have a significant negative effect if it is housed in a single area of the institution, separate from the central administration, and builds loyalty to that division. In that case, its university-wide responsibilities can disappear, and priorities for producing data sets and analysis may focus on a single aspect of the university, leaving others without support. While assignment within one division can be effective if university-wide products are regularly expected, the university-wide responsibilities of IR need emphasis and are best housed within the president's/chancellor's staff. By the way, it is also often true that IR is the institutional memory of the organization and that function also needs to be preserved.

In general, IR should regularly (annually or otherwise) publish statistical reports for the institution and needs to be structured in such a way as to be able to produce ad hoc reports as needed. Often, the president/chancellor is asked to respond quickly to legislative, donor, or other external constituencies and to internal governance groups, and IR needs to be able to produce the needed information in a timely fashion.

Role and Function

Most IR organizations are reactive rather than proactive, providing data and analysis only when requested. Throughout the organizations in any university, there is a need for "good" data on which to base decisions, a condition that is acute at the executive level. However, IR organizations, if left to their own devices, will collect and analyze only traditional data sets while institutional needs and challenges are changing.

As a result, it often occurs that institutions will collect and analyze data to satisfy the needs of external organizations such as boards of trustees and state and federal agencies, ignoring their own decisional imperatives. So it is necessary to encourage the IR component of the institution to be proactive, anticipating data and analysis needs based on the institution's condition and challenges.

Then the IR organization can become integral to policy and planning and in some cases leading those efforts. Thus, it is important to exercise great care in choosing leadership and staff of the IR organization and avoid transferring inferior administrators into these positions when they have not succeeded elsewhere in the institution.

Further, it is important to provide enough resources for travel to interact with other IR professionals as well as for continuing education. Otherwise, methodologies can become obsolete, and promising new methodologies for both collection and analysis might be overlooked or ignored.

Realize that your decisions, in general, should be data based. Using bad or inappropriate data may lead to questionable decisions, which in turn may lead to a shorter tenure.

NINE

In General

TRANSPARENCY, CONSULTATION, AND SHARED GOVERNANCE

There are no faculty at legitimate universities who do not believe that shared governance is not a God-given right. In fact, some believe that shared governance was one of the original Moses-purveyed commandments expunged by a malicious administrator at some point during Moses's journey down Mt. Sinai. However, defined reasonably, shared governance is a completely appropriate university value and practice.

"Defined reasonably" means that the definition fits a generally accepted definition as well as that of any reasonable person. And that concept is that before any major decision (and even some minor ones) is made, enough discussion occurs, interaction happens, and input is sought that those involved feel they have been heard. Following that consultation the person responsible for the decision decides and takes responsibility for it.

To some, shared governance means that once their opinion is expressed, their advice is followed. This is defining consultation unreasonably, and such a belief system afflicts many administrators, faculty, and staff, resulting in difficult times for an institution. Administrators working in this environment are automatically viewed by faculty and staff as autocratic, overbearing, and peremptory. And faculty and staff are seen by administrators as arrogant, overreaching, and disrespectful. Also, do not forget that shared governance includes students.

Operationalized, shared governance usually consists of administrators working with faculty, staff, and student committees to reach a decision or solve a problem. But no committee was ever fired because the solution failed or the decision was wrong. The administrators responsible were subject to that fate.

So a more appropriate view of shared governance in terms of administrative behavior includes gathering opinion from a spectrum of affected constituencies (consultation), considering that information, and reaching a decision or conclusion. That should also be the definition from a faculty, staff, or student perspective. And while the extent of consultation could be questioned or issue could be taken with the time taken to reach a conclusion, the final responsibility for the decision rests with the administrator.

Avoiding criticism over the extent of consultation is best handled by interacting with constituencies to determine how much is enough, in other words consulting about consulting. Agreeing beforehand won't guarantee that no one will take issue with your approach, but it will thin the opposing ranks. It will also go a long way toward developing your reputation for transparency.

Transparency has become a much sought after trait among administrators in both private and public entities. The expectation is that there will be openness, to the extent that no one's right to privacy is breached, and few hidden agendas and honesty will prevail.

The attractiveness of authentically engaging in transparent, consultative, shared governance is that, as a result, most individuals in the organization feel a part of the processes and are much more likely to buy in to the plans, goals, mission, values, and ethos of the organization. Transparency and consultation lead to shared governance, which in turn leads to shared values, goals, and vision for the institution.

Operationalizing Transparency

Several suggestions for operationalizing transparency and shared governance come to mind:

1. Define your view of shared governance and consultation early in your tenure. Share the definition in as many venues as prudent. As a result, there should be no confusion about your position.
2. Meet regularly and often with faculty, staff, and student leaders to discuss changes that might affect them.
3. Do not delegate important committee responsibilities. Attend personally and discuss impending changes before a decision is finalized.
4. Encourage direct reports to behave similarly.
5. In all cases, make clear that you are listening to all points of view.

DEALING WITH DIFFICULT PERSONALITIES

Universities are filled with people, employees, and students who, when their backs are against the wall, become difficult to deal with. Some are even difficult to deal with in the simplest of day-to-day interactions. But almost all university types are intelligent and articulate, think critically, and have a highly developed sense of affront and injustice. So everyone has the potential to be a difficult personality in one situation or another.

The first rule in dealing with difficult personalities is to remain calm, much the same as you would when dealing with an emergency. In many interpersonally difficulty situations, the difficult party usually thrives on your reaction. If you raise your voice, panic, or overreact in any number of ways, that party has achieved his or her goal.

Second, deflect attacks with accurate data. Prepare carefully for any meeting that could be difficult by being better prepared than any of your opponents. When that tactic fails and you are not fully prepared, admit to not having the data at hand. Offer to read whatever your adversary might offer to better understand the situation. The offer gains time for you and obviates the necessity for offering answers before all the facts are known.

Next try to avoid surprises such as confrontations in public places, chance meetings with opponents, and meetings concerning other subjects where an opponent might surface an unrelated topic. Of course, these situations are sometimes unavoidable, so when they occur, remember the first and second rules.

And finally, always be prepared to extricate yourself from chance encounters by pleading sickness, pressing business, or general overprogramming. Small misdirections such as these are easily forgiven if you get caught.

BEHAVIORS OF DIFFICULT PERSONALITIES

Dealing with constituents who have difficult and confrontational personalities and oppose either you and/or your policies and goals can be both time consuming and dangerous. Nothing pleases an opponent more than your overreaction to a situation that he or she has concocted or your inability to respond to a challenge. On every campus, there are individuals who do not support a leader's goals, and their intelligence and guile make their behavior especially vexing.

Several of the more common behaviors are worth noting:

1. A faculty member joins you at a committee meeting carrying a stack of papers purported to document your statements contradicting the committee's goals. Always offer to read the documents outside the committee meeting, in order to respond later. Odds are, you will never receive the documents.
2. A constituent heckles you during a speech. First, ignore the interruption. When your patience runs out, respond in a measured way, offering to discuss the issues in a different forum or at a later

time. In general, do not try to respond humorously because you're bound to offend someone and you might turn the crowd against you. Never respond arrogantly or personally attack the heckler. He or she might respond more cleverly than you.
3. When rumors about you or your colleagues or family come to your attention, ignore them, unless they are reporting illegal behavior. If illegal behavior is reported, investigate. If there is no illegal behavior, ignore them, unless you believe that exoneration is in order. Then find a way to respond professionally.
4. When attacked in print or visual media, ignore the insult. The news cycle is short and memories are even shorter.
5. When confronted individually in a public place, respond in a friendly, understanding way. Your behavior will often disarm the attacker.

In general, intelligent opponents are attempting to elicit a response that will support their position and grow in the telling. Your goal is to minimize the damage, not crush your attacker. Crushing the opponent will not enhance your reputation, although it may provide you some satisfaction.

DEALING WITH SENSITIVE SITUATIONS

Every campus endures crisis situations at some time. And whether the campus emerges stronger or weaker at crisis conclusion often depends on how the president/chancellor handles the situation. Consider for example several types of crisis situations.

Budget crises have become common. Whether inflation has gotten the best of an institution, enrollment shortfalls have taken their toll, or a natural disaster has required an unexpected capital investment, acceptable solutions are crafted only with strong and visible leadership. In these situations, the president/chancellor must determine whether careful planning has made a quick and painless solution manifest or the intellectual resources of the campus must be marshaled to deal with the problem. In the latter case, the character of the crisis must be assessed and a decision made whether a tactical or strategic approach is appropriate.

But whether tactical or strategic or some combination of both, the president/chancellor must be the organizer and leader of the effort, involving as many campus constituencies in the process as possible. In this way, the solution has a high probability of garnering campus buy-in, no matter how painful the solution, if the campus CEO has been deeply involved in the effort and the campus itself is stronger as a result.

Internally generated campus crises are also common, such as the following examples:

1. A campus group is energized by a national, state, or local decision and decides that the campus must be involved.
2. An administrative decision such as tuition increase is so unpopular as to result in widespread protest.
3. A grave injustice is perceived by a campus group resulting in the group's taking public action.

In each of these situations, the potential for adverse publicity is high, and the campus turns to the CEO for leadership.

Especially important in this type of confrontation is the visible presence of the president/chancellor. Delegating responsibility to any other campus functionary will be a sign of weakness, and whatever resolution eventually results, the president will be criticized for failing as a leader. So the president/chancellor must deal continually and directly with the aggrieved parties and employ the best of common sense to reach a resolution.

A third type of crisis results from a disaster, accident, or crime occurring on campus. A murder or rape occurs. A fire guts a room, several rooms, or a building. A student is hurt or killed in a pedestrian encounter with an automobile. Again, each of these situations requires direct involvement of the president/chancellor lest an accusation of insensitivity, lack of caring, wrong priorities, or poor leadership be leveled at the CEO.

The common denominator in all of these situations is leader involvement. When bad things occur on campus, get in the middle of them. Be visible. Be caring. Be a leader!

Not a Crisis but Still Difficult

Difficult and uncomfortable situations that do not rise to the level of a campus crisis will be commonplace during a president's/chancellor's tenure. It is not possible to deal with all of them, but you can be sure that you will be judged on your behavior and attendance. Several are worthy of discussion.

Deaths of students, faculty, and staff and their loved ones present a special challenge. Some institutions are so large that it will be impossible to know about, much less attend, funerals or other formal acknowledgments of a passing. However, on most campuses, the numbers are not as daunting.

Where faculty and staff are concerned, always attend funerals for them or close relatives. And always acknowledge the event with a sympathy card and/or flora. Be especially careful not to discriminate with respect to likes and dislikes or position in the organization. Deaths are traumatic for everyone and your attention will be appreciated.

Where students are concerned, attend any student funeral. Be sure to seek out parents and close relatives to express your feelings directly.

Where relatives of students are concerned, acknowledge a passing with a written expression of sympathy whenever you learn of the event. Realize that you won't know about all of them.

Several acutely uncomfortable situations bear description. Imagine a faculty member complaining that his father's death was not acknowledged when he hid news of the event in order to cause campus unrest. Imagine a president/chancellor participating in an argument about campus politics at a calling or funeral. Imagine a campus executive's parent's passing remaining unacknowledged by system officials. These situations and others create great consternation and are easily avoided.

Invitations to social events and official functions can also generate uncomfortable situations. Extreme care must be taken not to base guest lists on personal preferences. Similar care must be taken to ensure that your interactions at events and functions are not based on your personal likes and dislikes. Like it or not, you are the president/chancellor 24/7, and your behavior in social situations will color your reputation for equanimity on campus.

Lying can also create uncomfortable situations. Avoid lying at all costs. However, some lies are unavoidable. Protecting a colleague, ensuring confidentiality, or adhering to a legal document can all be a basis for being untruthful; however, if such lying is employed regularly, colleagues will not know when and what to believe.

Being caught in a significant lie can bias your entire tenure. Your best protection is to be truthful and, failing that, be apologetic and remorseful and beg forgiveness. By the way, a significant fraction of campus executives tailor responses to what they believe their audiences want to hear. The tactic can be successful in the short run, but will fail over time.

Students bringing personal or academic problems directly to the president/chancellor can also create uncomfortable situations. Problems can be minimized by your having an on-campus administrative colleague who can be trusted not only to investigate problems thoroughly but also to execute solutions for those that are legitimate. Having a trusted troubleshooter is invaluable.

On every campus, the president/chancellor has supporters and detractors. Ambling across campus, a president/chancellor will encounter both. While it is almost impossible to treat them equally, it is extremely important to be acutely aware of your own behavior as you attempt to be evenhanded in your interaction. It is not an exaggeration to state that every interaction will be noted and judged.

APPEARING TO BE ALL THINGS TO ALL PEOPLE

The president/chancellor of any academic institution serves multiple constituencies—students, faculty and staff, donors, appointed and elected officials, alumni, community organizations, foundation executives, and boards of trustees, to name a few. Developing a relationship with this disparate set of groups can be daunting, at best. It requires bridging gaps (or at least appearing to bridge gaps) between liberals and conservatives, wealthy and needy, Republicans and Democrats, students and faculty, the sciences and humanities, and the artistic and the philistine, among many others. So the president/chancellor must indeed be all things to all people to be successful.

Accomplishing this kind of universality demands moderation, consistency, constancy, dogged belief in the institution and its mission, unswerving respect for points of view different from your own, and unassailable integrity. If you have extreme beliefs, express them in moderate ways. Remain consistent in that expression because if you purvey one point of view to a group and an inconsistent viewpoint to another, when they compare notes (and they surely will), your reputation for honesty is at risk. If a group disagrees with your approach, respectfully continue discussion until you're sure that each side fully understands the other's position. Agreeing to disagree is a reasonable outcome to a discussion, as long as respect and integrity are retained. Communication with constituencies must be constant and continual to send the message that your commitment to the institution and its mission is always the basis for your actions and you care deeply about your beliefs. Of course, respect for those participating in the conversation must always be maintained, and the quality and content of your message must be such that your integrity is never questioned.

Being all things to all people really means that in any conversation, those involved reach a point where all sides understand the message, respect the sender, and maintain their integrity throughout the process.

BEING A ROLE MODEL

From the moment a new president/chancellor is named, that person is carefully observed, scrutinized, judged, and discussed by everyone he or she meets or encounters. He or she finds that every behavior is the subject of public and individual opinion and discussion. And reputations rise and fall on that basis. Further, the tenor of those opinions determines the quality of future personal and professional interactions and ultimately determines the success or failure of the campus CEO.

Each institution claims a set of values, usually enumerated in its strategic plan and distributed in its publications, presentations, and media releases. Usually included are integrity, transparency, civility, and equity. Those values must be embodied and constantly modeled by the president/chancellor to maintain a personal and professional reputation and, more importantly, ensure the reputation of the institution.

Within the institution, no group experiences the behavior of the president/chancellor more often and closely than direct reports. And it is these individuals who are expected to lead in accomplishing the daily business of the organization. Nothing erodes the effectiveness of a leadership team faster than a president/chancellor behaving in ways or expecting behavior that contradicts the values of the institution. Further, a leader's toxic behavior (berating, belittling, publicly criticizing) can have a chilling effect on subordinates' ability to do their jobs. And no matter how professionally the direct reports act, the president's or chancellor's reputation will be known on and off campus.

Behavior in general campus interactions is similar. Based on the premise that every job is important (custodian, faculty, or administrator), interactions on campus must be pleasant, attentive, and respectful. It requires little energy and reaps massive rewards to ask a clerical or service person how the day is going and to listen to the answer. Similarly, remembering names is a sign of respect and will be returned in kind.

In campus meetings, responding angrily to a challenge is anathema. Develop a set of responses that are not confronting, but are responsive. Possibilities are "I'm not familiar with the details of that situation. If you would provide me with them later, I'll be glad to respond" or "The time allotted for this forum does not allow for a satisfactory response. Perhaps we could discuss the issue in another venue." Of course situations are sufficiently varied that one will encounter those where no response is deemed adequate. Rest assured, however, an angry response is always counterproductive.

In the community external to campus, similar rules apply. Most communities expect the campus CEO to be presidential but approachable, confident and resolute but sensitive, brilliant but having common sense. In most communities, the campus CEO is not only the face of the campus but also the embodiment of the campus. Thus, institutional values and the CEO's values must be the same.

Any negative interaction with a shopkeeper, involvement in a questionable business deal, service on the board of a company or bank of questionable reputation, or dispute on campus that becomes public can endanger the CEO's reputation and effectiveness. Expectations are high and should be.

Presidents/chancellors are expected to be nothing less than superpeople. And since campuses and communities are filled with bright, articulate people and critiquing leaders has become a national sport, they can afford to aspire to no less.

A List of Role-Model Don'ts

Being the campus role model requires constant attention and attendant constancy. Imagine the reputation of a campus CEO and the expected behavior of others on campus if the following were true:

1. The president/chancellor dresses unprofessionally, is unkempt, and often wears the colors of rival institutions.
2. Minor mistakes invite public castigation by the campus CEO.
3. The president/chancellor berates, discounts, and demeans service persons in community businesses.
4. At athletic events, the president/chancellor screams at referees and players from the stands.
5. Both on campus and in the community, the president/chancellor is serially untruthful.
6. At campus meetings, the president/chancellor loudly, aggressively, and threateningly accosts those who disagree with him or her.
7. The president/chancellor has no time for students, except for the children or relatives of major donors.
8. The president/chancellor takes little responsibility for policies on campus and delegates almost all signature authority.
9. The president/chancellor is seldom seen outside his or her office and does not attend campus events.

Any one of these behaviors could empower the campus population to behave similarly and inappropriately. All of these behaviors are destructive to institutional cohesion and progress.

TAKING AND CASTING THE BLAME

Responsibility for everything that happens at a university rests with the president/chancellor. That doesn't mean that the CEO takes the blame for anything and everything, but it does mean that responsibility for some part of every incident (positive or negative) resides in that office. And whether it's lack of oversight, direct involvement in a wrong decision, a bad hire, shortfalls in policy infrastructure, or just being at the wrong place at the wrong time, it can be argued that the CEO is not blameless.

But in any situation, if the president/chancellor acts as the primary representative of the institution, its public face, his or her reputation will be enhanced, unless the CEO is directly involved in felonious behavior or takes obviously ill-advised positions. Standing up for the university, acting as its primary spokesperson, being the embodiment of the institution, and taking responsibility only improves the reputation of the institution's leader. In that way, the institution's constituencies can identify the strength of leadership, the fact that the university is being led, and that someone is at least accepting some part of the blame. Make no mistake, people need someone to blame.

In addition, the simplest and most effective two words that a leader can intone are "I'm sorry!" Those two words cover a spectrum of sins and are usually accepted when sincerely offered. In short, accepting responsibility is widely respected.

On the other hand, casting the blame is not. It's one thing to blame external forces and constituencies and circumstances, but even there, blaming others is widely construed as a sign of weakness. And while casting the blame externally is not incredibly dangerous, it is often seen as shirking responsibility.

Blaming subordinates, however, is incredibly dangerous. Not only is it bad form to blame people within an organization for which you are responsible, but such behavior causes your subordinates to question your loyalty to them and, by extension, their loyalty to you. Throwing anyone under the bus invites the question "Who's next?"

BLAME TAKING AS A TACTIC

Accepting responsibility for all that occurs on a university campus is a time-honored means of expressing leadership. However, that act can engender much more extensive and unexpected effects. It can enhance the feeling of security on campus. It can enhance community support for the campus. It can indicate loyalty to the institution and to individuals. And it can massively enhance the reputation of the president/chancellor.

Do not, however, confuse taking responsibility for difficult issues with taking credit for positive events. Embrace the former. Avoid the latter.

When problematic events occur, your accepting responsibility not only gives notice to both the university and external community that you are leading but also announces that you intend to protect the campus and its occupants from future threats. Stated appropriately, it will also give notice that those directly responsible will be treated justly. In that way, campus citizens are helped to feel more secure.

Accepting responsibility allows the external community to feel that the negative event occurring on campus will not be allowed to spill over into the community. Further, if the event directly affects both campus and community, steps will be taken to ensure nonrecurrence.

When other campus officials might have been implicated in the event, your taking responsibility allows them the space to accept their part of the responsibility. It is also an indication that those not responsible will not be blamed. It can also carry an implication of loyalty to the campus, involved individuals, and those not involved. And it is axiomatic that your loyalty will be repaid in kind.

As a result, in these situations, your calm, evenhanded, responsible behavior will establish and enhance positive aspects of your reputation.

However, a competing reaction will occur if you cast the blame on others and take little or no responsibility for the problematic event. Similarly, if you take credit for positive events such as athletic successes, scientific breakthroughs, and intellectual triumphs, that act will engender opposite reactions, and you and your reputation will suffer.

HIRING AND FIRING

Accession and retention policies and practices shape the character of institutions in several ways. Most obvious in this regard is the quality of faculty and staff. Maintaining rigorous hiring standards and separating underperforming and countercultural employees from the institution are important to building the reputation of the institution both internally and externally. However, other considerations are also important.

When positions within the institution become vacant, how they are filled can have a profound effect on faculty and staff attitudes. Specifically, filling a position internally sends a message that current employees are respected and current, upwardly mobile employees can access a productive career path within the organization. If, on the other hand, for the sake of institutional improvement or because needed skill sets are not available within the current pool of employees, it is deemed necessary to hire externally, employee morale may suffer and institutional culture can change. When hiring externally, reasoning should be communicated clearly.

So it is important to strike a balance between internal and external accessions that fits institutional culture. And the balance may shift from one side to the other, depending on institutional size, financial circumstances, and conditions at the moment.

Faculty and professional positions in colleges and universities are ordinarily filled using a process that includes a search committee established by choosing from among individuals representing affected constituencies. Sometimes these committees are small (three to five), especially in situations where the position has limited purview, or fairly large (twenty-five to thirty) where a search for a president/chancellor is necessary.

Whatever the position and size of the committee, it is critical to reach an understanding that the committee only advises the hiring authority and that its result is strictly a recommendation. It is, however, extremely important that the hiring authority listen carefully to what the search committee recommends. In instances when the advice is not followed, be direct and clear about why. Finally, never forget to thank them for their work.

Skilled staff positions are often filled using a process overseen by the institutional human resources organization. Often, a choice is made from a pool of applicants after interviews have been conducted.

Whatever process is employed, there must be a perception of fairness throughout the organization and among external constituencies. Ultimately, the president/chancellor is responsible for ensuring that perception.

Separating employees from the university presents similar risks and rewards. Continuing to employ underperformers can have deleterious effects on the performance of adequate and high-performing personnel, risk institutional reputation, and increase institutional liabilities, both legal and financial.

Even more dangerous is continuing to employ those whose behavior is countercultural or in direct opposition to the values of the organization. Countercultural behaviors might include inability to work in teams, belittling and/or demeaning and/or disrespecting colleagues, creating a hostile work environment, and inability to behave collegially, among others. Behavior contrary to institutional values is more obvious and includes theft, sexual harassment and assault, alcohol- and drug-related offenses, and other illegal acts.

Continuing to employ those behaving counterculturally and/or in opposition to institutional values puts at risk not only the internal and external reputation of the institution but also its financial well-being. Both are critical, because the internal and external constituencies determine the performance and financial health of the institution.

Separating an individual from an institution requires care in following the established procedures. The most common cause for reversal of an employee's layoff, furlough, firing, suspension, or other adverse employment act is not following established standards and procedures, thereby denying the employee due process. And reversal of one of your decisions, especially by an external organization, is not good for your reputation. A good human resources professional can protect you from this threat, but you must learn the rules and use your own common sense to best avoid the risk.

The greater risk to you is the perception that continuing employees will have of your part in the separation. Following the established rules helps, but the rumors that result from the separation of any employee from an institution, for good or bad reasons, circulate quickly and can be destructive. Employees' rights to privacy make it very difficult to defend the institution's reputation or your own. It is in these situations where a thick skin, open communication, good media relations, and security in the knowledge that you have acted correctly are your protection.

Pitfalls in the Employment Process

Accession, retention, and rejection of employees at universities results in anxiety and disruption unmatched in most other institutions. Of course, most other institutions are neither as conservative nor as resistant to change as most universities. Most do not become mired in the process of change as do universities, and most do not have the intellectual capacity for concocting rumors and engaging in conspiracy theory.

Filling vacant positions encourages anxiety, whether the hire is internal or external. While budget considerations may dictate the need for an internal search and filling positions internally signals confidence in current employees' abilities, the process may create unhealthy competition among colleagues and ruin cohesion in an otherwise smoothly functioning team. On the other hand, hiring externally can invite anxiety-producing situations, as CVs of applicants are compared to those of current employees and personalities of current and potential employees are analyzed for cultural fit.

A process that is open and transparent will help to ease this discomfort, but it cannot be completely avoided. And while the details of academic and administrative searches are easily opened to scrutiny, searches for clerical and service staff positions are often handled by HR organizations, which tend to be much less transparent. Encouraging transparency in hiring throughout the institution is your best option.

The ultimate goal of any hiring process should be to fill vacancies with the best possible applicant who is a cultural fit and will remain with the institution. Too many administrators approach hiring with the idea that if the hire doesn't work out, the process is easily repeated. That attitude is costly to the university not only because both the search process and retraining are expensive but also because the effort itself drains emotion and energy. Your hiring goal should be 100 percent long-term employees.

Evaluation of current employees is similarly problematic. In academic institutions, most faculty, staff, and administrators pathologically avoid assessments, citing complicated and unfathomable job requirements, heterogeneous client populations, and unstable environments. However, funders, donors, students, internal clients, and society are demanding accountability, and it begins with individual assessments.

The institution's responsibility in this situation is to provide authenticated evaluation tools and an environment and process that are deemed fair by those involved. It is also important that evaluations are viewed as formative rather than summative. Only in rare situations should the evaluative process result in termination.

In academic institutions, student evaluations of faculty, faculty evaluations of administrators, and client evaluations of providers are common. While it is often the case that those being evaluated are uncomfortable with the process and the concept, the results of these evaluations can be useful in performance improvement. However, the form and process of the evaluations should be monitored to ensure fairness and protect individual privacy rights where necessary.

When termination becomes necessary, ensure that institutional processes and policies are carefully followed. Do not involve yourself in levels of the process where your presence is not officially required.

In hiring, individual assessment, and employee termination, your behavior and involvement with your direct reports and staff will be the model for the rest of the campus. Your handling of those situations will be microscopically analyzed and the subject of discussions across campus. Act accordingly!

BUDGET AND FINANCE

College and university budgets are among the most carefully studied institutional documents. The details contained in the documents are well known to the institutional financial affairs organizations, internal audit, and senate committees and subcommittees as well as union officials, external auditors, and the press. For public institutions, they are also scrutinized by legislators, legislative staffs, and state agencies. Institutional finances are important.

Appointment as president/chancellor means that you assume all of the financial challenges faced by the institution. You can't duck or delegate them because resourcing the institution is one of your primary responsibilities. So whether the institution is experiencing budget surpluses, shortfalls, or making budget, you are saddled with the burden.

If the institution is enjoying a budget surplus, use that opportunity to expand contingency and reserve funds because a shortfall will certainly occur in the future. Save part of the surplus to fund projects that are unexpected targets of opportunity or unfunded priorities. Or expand funding to especially worthy projects. Ensure that the distribution is related to the institution's strategic plan.

However, above all, make sure that campus constituencies believe that funds are distributed equitably and rationally, departments have the funding to address their primary mission, worthy projects receive adequate support, and campus constituencies are satisfied with the process. The last condition is satisfied through consultation so that all involved believe they are a part of the process and the process has been transparent throughout.

Transparency and inclusion are especially important (critical) if the institution faces a budget shortfall. In this situation, the entire campus becomes consumed in worry about who or what will be cut. Faculty will immediately point out that no teaching function should be decremented, and many presidents/chancellors will fall prey to this argument, choosing to discontinue student services, cut back campus maintenance and support staff, and decrease general-fund support to athletics and recreation.

However, it is important to quickly and carefully study the causes of the budget problems, involving as much of the campus as possible in the study. If cuts are necessary, assuming a strategic rather than a tactical approach will serve you well. Choosing to make across-the-board cuts (a tactical move at best) will result in accusations of sloth and even a couple of mortal sins.

Take enough time and expend enough energy to ensure that cuts are related to the strategic plan and institutional mission, and especially to the root causes of the shortfall. If the shortfall is caused by enrollment decreases, the campus must be led to the idea that some teaching functions will be decremented. If inflation and/or rising costs are creating the problem, then teaching functions might be protected but can be affected if the situation warrants.

Whatever the chosen solution, the goal is for campus constituencies to feel involved and believe that the chosen solution is rational, whether or not they agree with it.

At the same time that cuts are being contemplated, it falls to the president/chancellor to explore expanding current funding streams and/or finding new ones. Inclusiveness is important in this process also. And whether the solutions include expanding enrollment, seeking more public support, relying on greater donor generosity, or applying for more grants and contracts, the CEO must be the visible leader in the effort.

Budget and Finance Tips

Some specific pieces of advice are useful in dealing with budget issues whether or not the campus is facing challenges:

1. Share financial information widely with campus constituencies.
2. Include all formal budget committees in the discussions.
3. Ensure that all decisions are rational and defensible.
4. When cuts are necessary, avoid layoffs, to the extent possible. Cut vacant positions, not individuals.
5. If conditions change, share the information immediately.
6. Lead visibly, but distance yourself to avoid accusations of playing favorites.

COMMUNICATION

College and university campuses are filled with intelligent, articulate, and well-educated people. Often, even the clerical and service personnel and custodians have earned degrees. As a result, they will engage in discussions of campus issues at a surprisingly sophisticated level, suggesting solutions that are not only practical and useful but also not previously concocted by you and your immediate staff. So broad consultation can be very productive. However, it works and yields positive contributions only if those involved are well informed.

Most commonly, campus constituencies are not well informed, and their intelligence and education take them to the dark side. Lacking facts, they will imagine doomsday scenarios and pass along rumors that may make solutions to problems impossible and your position untenable. When a crisis occurs, your best defense is openness, transparency, directness, and a history of sharing information. If you have been sharing information all along, even when there were no campus issues, your constituencies will be more likely to listen during a crisis period.

So when a campus issue, problem, or crisis occurs, deal with it directly. Use whatever means available to distribute information as quickly and seamlessly as possible, realizing that there may be legal limits to the information you can share. And when legal limitations are in play, explain them to the best of your ability. Whatever happens, do not put yourself in the position of having to explain misdirection or a lie. Memories are long and acceptance of your future utterances is at risk.

Even when the campus is running smoothly, distributing information is important. Newsletters, announcements, minutes of meetings, and other print-based mechanisms are useful, but they can too easily be discarded before being read and are often ignored in the press of daily business. Social media can be effective for informing students, but faculty and staff are often not as electronically adept or interested.

Other means are often more effective. Walk around campus and talk to people. Encourage your immediate staff to act similarly. Discuss campus issues no matter how uncomfortable, and do not avoid subjects introduced by those you meet. In meetings and when appropriate, bring up subjects about which you believe those present should be informed. Invite faculty and staff to informal meetings, and encourage them to discuss any subject of interest to them. Word-of-mouth transmission of information can be very effective.

In these ways, you develop a reputation for universally sharing information so that when a crisis occurs, you have proven lines of communication and broad bandwidth to utilize.

Communication with off-campus constituencies should follow a similar pattern. Attend as many meetings as possible, and develop a reputation for openness and willingness to share information. Be visible and open at community functions. Always respond to press inquiries. Form a community advisory board, which can help you tailor ways to inform the public and transmit your message.

In general, the more people on and off campus know, the less the campus will be affected by rumor, innuendo, and outright falsehoods.

Communication Tips

Several bits of advice might be useful in developing an approach to communication:

1. Within legal and ethical limits, share information widely.
2. Tailor communication mechanisms to the constituencies involved. For students, use social and electronic media. For faculty and staff, use electronic and print media. For external constituencies, use print and visual media. For small, influential groups such as the board, use personal letters and contact.
3. As much as feasible, walk around and engage in face-to-face interactions. Hold receptions and small group meetings to disseminate information by word of mouth.
4. Organize small, randomly selected discussion groups to meet regularly with you to disseminate information as well as to allow them to assess you personally.
5. Realize that overexposure is not possible where you're concerned. You are the face of the university. Act like it.

AN IMPORTANT PARTNERSHIP AND COMMITMENT

From the moment a campus leader signs his or her employment contract, whether contractually stated or not, an expectation is created that the new executive's spouse or partner will become integral to campus life and his or her commitment to the institution is no less than 24/7.

That a spouse or partner will participate as fully as possible is a given since most boards and institutions believe that they are hiring a team. And whether it is attendance at receptions, formal dinners, athletics contests, lectures, donor interactions, or any of the broad range of events occurring regularly on a campus, absences will be noted. Often, when events occur simultaneously, duties can be split.

Similarly, hosting events is a team effort, where both of you are expected to be involved. Also, realize that a spouse or partner may be subject to specific responsibilities of his or her own. Included might be leading some fund-raising efforts, hosting campus-specific clubs, and entertaining the spouses and partners of visiting dignitaries.

Whatever the expectations, it is important to discuss them during contract negotiations so there are no surprises and no unforgivable sins are committed by you or the institution.

Finally, and most important, realize that your commitment to the institution is 24/7. As leader of the institution, you are the institution, and you must always be available when needed. And your behavior, as well as that of your family, will be under constant scrutiny during your tenure.

TEN

Case Studies

Following are two descriptions of events that illustrate the breadth of constituencies involved when difficulties occur on campus and some means of dealing with them.

CORPUS CHRISTI: A CHALLENGE TO ACADEMIC AND PERSONAL FREEDOM

In the spring of 2001, two state senators visited the chancellor of Indiana University–Purdue University Fort Wayne (IPFW) unannounced, stating that they had heard that the IPFW theater department was producing a play that was both defamatory to Christians and, in their opinion, blasphemous. They demanded that the chancellor stop production of the play, or they would introduce legislation to reduce funding to the university. The chancellor, knowing none of the details surrounding the allegations nor anything about the play, agreed to check into the matter. The senators departed with a promise that the chancellor would get back to them. Neither the chancellor nor the senators had read the play.

Upon checking into the senators' allegations, the chancellor discovered that a directing student had proposed producing and directing the play *Corpus Christi*, written by Terrence McNally, as an independent project during his junior year. He was told that he lacked the requisite experience for the undertaking, whereupon he spent his junior year taking appropriate seminars and classes and his proposal was accepted by the department as his senior project. The play was scheduled to be presented in August. The student solicited private donations and successfully funded the project.

The play centers on a homosexual, mid-twenties character born in Corpus Christi, Texas, who gathers twelve gay disciples around him. It is an allegorical comedy that retells the story of Christ from a gay perspective. At that time, it had been produced only once before.

Further, northeast Indiana, where IPFW is located, is a conservative Republican stronghold. It is also host to a broad array of conservative Christian religious groups including (but not limited to) Mennonites, Amish, Evangelicals, Baptists, and both sects of Lutherans.

From the moment he learned that the project had been accepted by the theater department, the chancellor, on behalf of the university, believed that production of the play was protected under the aegis of academic freedom and freedom of speech and expression. And he communicated that belief to the senators.

The senators responded by enlisting four of their colleagues who co-signed a letter published in the *Fort Wayne Journal Gazette*, decrying presentation of the play, demanding that it be canceled, and calling the chancellor cowardly, hypocritical, and anti-Christian, but stepped away from their threats to reduce funding to the university. The chancellor then published an op-ed piece explaining in detail the university's position, the meaning of academic freedom, and the place of universities in society and explained that the production would not be canceled.

During the intervening months between the public revelation that the play would be produced and the actual production of the play, multiple related skirmishes occurred.

Several hundred e-mail and US mail messages were sent to the institution. Most criticized the university as blasphemous and made various demands. All received replies in the same form as their transmission, some tailored to the sender, some generic. All were signed by the chancellor.

Approximately three hundred phone calls on the subject were made to the university switchboard. Most were taken immediately or were returned by either the chancellor, the vice-chancellor for academic affairs, or the executive director of university relations. In nearly all cases, conversations that began angrily ended rationally with an agreement to disagree or an understanding of both proponents' viewpoints.

Several callers and writers threatened donations to the university; however, on investigation, it was found that the vast majority had never given, and the rest had given only small amounts.

The chancellor accepted numerous speaking engagements and interviews locally and around the region to explain the mission, values, and position of the university. One area Rotary Club rescinded an invitation to speak, citing the institution's anti-Christian behavior. The chancellor received an invitation to appear on *The O'Reilly Factor*, which he declined due to the pugnacious nature of the host.

Both the chancellor and the theater department head received death threats, and the chancellor's home was decorated with raw eggs.

Multiple campus forums were organized to express and expose the competing viewpoints. Many local clergy participated, as did many IPFW faculty, staff, and students.

A federal lawsuit was filed by several local citizens seeking to restrain the university from producing the play. After the local federal judge ruled in favor of the university, the case was appealed to the Seventh Circuit Court, which also ruled in favor of the university.

Negotiations with the National Catholic League and its president, Bill Donohue, led to an agreement that its literature and a statement would be distributed in the theater lobby. No other religious organization or sect asked for such an accommodation.

The governor's office requested six tickets to the production.

The story was followed and carried by several national news outlets.

The play opened in August. Although student projects were traditionally scheduled for only one performance and played to a parent-populated audience, the play was scheduled for six performances, all of which sold out. All six of the governor's tickets were used.

Following guidelines for such situations, the university set aside areas for protest, both pro and con. Only on the night of the last performance was the con area used, and the protestors were courteous, respectful, and nondestructive.

While the entire situation was uncomfortable and disruptive to university function, it proved to be very valuable to the institution. The university fulfilled its mission by educating the community about the role of the university in society and in the Fort Wayne community. Whether on one side or the other of the question of the play's worth or appropriateness, faculty, staff, and students came together to defend their university and the freedom of thought and expression defined in its values. So as never before, IPFW came together as a university and attained a self-image and level of self-worth that would have been unattainable in any other way.

MURDER ON CAMPUS: DEALING WITH A DIFFICULT EVENT

In the spring of 2008, a female student was stabbed to death in IPFW student housing.

IPFW student housing consisted of one-, two-, and four-bedroom apartments in which students occupied single bedrooms and no more than two people shared a bathroom. Men and women could not share apartments and alcohol was not allowed. Nonresidents were required to register if staying overnight.

The stabbing occurred in a four-bedroom unit and was discovered by a roommate who entered the apartment from the hallway and found only the victim present. The death was initially reported to the campus police as a suicide. After an initial investigation that resulted in the police declaring it a homicide, a cautionary statement was distributed electronically throughout the campus. The victim was an exchange student from New Mexico State University who had come to IPFW for a single semester.

Since the campus police lacked the experience and forensic capabilities to investigate such a crime, the Fort Wayne Police Department was called in. A long-standing mutual support agreement served as the basis for collaboration. Interviews were conducted with involved parties, and it was determined that another roommate's mother, who had been staying in the apartment as an unregistered guest, was the primary suspect.

By this time, local media had learned of the incident and were present on campus and attempting to interview anyone they could find. One newsperson climbed through a window of the restricted building and was escorted out by law enforcement. Further electronic updates were sent to campus constituencies. The campus was never closed.

The parents of the victim and her university were notified and the chancellor and vice-chancellor for student affairs called the parents and officials of the home university. Grief counselors were called in to support IPFW students and staff, and multiple meetings were held to allow those affected to express their feelings and correct any misinformation that was being shared.

Within twenty-four hours, the suspect was apprehended in another Indiana city. She was brought back to Fort Wayne and admitted that she had stabbed the victim in a fit of rage resulting from comments the victim had made about her daughter. She also had a history of drug abuse.

Community members who had begun describing the campus as a violent place, were called by the chancellor and vice-chancellors in an effort to define the episode as a random and isolated act of violence that had occurred under almost unreproducible circumstances. Multiple interviews were granted to newspapers, radio, and television outlets to describe the event accurately.

Several campus events were arranged including candlelight vigils, forums, and religious services, at which multiple university officials were present. The extensive communications efforts calmed the campus very quickly.

The family of the victim was not able to come to Fort Wayne immediately but traveled to campus subsequently and met with the chancellor and other university officials. In spite of a local lawyer encouraging the family to file a wrongful death suit against the university, the support and sympathy shown by the campus caused the family to ask only that a scholarship be established in the student's name. The scholarship was funded, and the family remains friendly to the campus.

Housing regulations were tightened as a result of the incident; however, it remains unclear whether the changes would have prevented the event. No lasting effects of the homicide were obvious.

Conclusion

Being successful as a president/chancellor requires a multidimensional array of talents. Those talents include but are not limited to the ability to be interpersonally comfortable, analytical, visionary, assertive, compelling in public presentations, and flexible and represent the institution as a role model and its public face. The challenge for many campus leaders is that they come to the positions having only a few of these abilities. And where the abilities are absent, training is required, or parts of the job are poorly done.

Consider the loss of campus and community respect and support in the following situations:

1. The president/chancellor is a brilliant orator and an able fund-raiser, especially for construction projects, and has legislative connections that guarantee employee salary enhancements every year. However, he or she is so aggressive that students and employees fear him or her and he or she is involved with ethically questionable projects off campus.
2. Constituents consider the president/chancellor generally capable, but his or her spouse/partner continually and publicly criticizes the campus and the community, both on and off campus.
3. Interpersonally, the president/chancellor is outstanding, showing care and concern for employees and students as well as community needs. However, he or she has little vision for the campus and its programs to the extent that there has been no updating to construction or facilities in years.
4. The president/chancellor is gifted at satisfying board needs, which include slavish protection of the status quo. Campus growth and development are largely ignored because the campus leader is uncomfortable dealing with donors and legislators.
5. Constituent groups generally support the leader's ideas for the physical and programmatic development of the campus, but the leader is uncomfortable at public gatherings and a poor public speaker, causing ideas to be misunderstood and misinterpreted by those who do not know him or her well.

In many of these cases, recognition that weaknesses exist and a willingness to seek help in overcoming them can significantly improve performance. However, arrogance and ego often trump good judgment and realistic assessment.

Careful assessment of the job requirements and your collection of talents and abilities immediately as you assume the position and continually throughout your tenure will serve you well. Further, your willingness to heed the results and improve your performance will help to ensure your success on behalf of the institution. At the very least, your running against the wind will become easier.

www.ingramcontent.com/pod-product-compliance
Lightning Source LLC
Chambersburg PA
CBHW021800230426
43669CB00006B/150